Two Forms of Conservatism

Two Forms of Conservatism

Judicial Reasoning in New York Courts,
1860–1920

William E. Nelson

University Press of Kansas

Published by the University Press of Kansas (Lawrence, Kansas 66045), which was organized by the Kansas Board of Regents and is operated and funded by Emporia State University, Fort Hays State University, Kansas State University, Pittsburg State University, the University of Kansas, and Wichita State University.

Library of Congress Cataloging-in-Publication Data

Names: Nelson, William E., author.
Title: Two forms of conservatism : judicial reasoning in New York Courts, 1860–1920 / William E. Nelson.
Description: Lawrence : University Press of Kansas, 2024. | Includes index.
Identifiers: LCCN 2023044355 (print) | LCCN 2023044356 (ebook)
ISBN 9780700636648 (cloth)
ISBN 9780700636655 (ebook)
Subjects: LCSH: Judicial process—New York (State)—History. | Justice, Administration of—New York (State)—History. | Courts—New York (State)—History. | Conservatism—New York (State)—History.
Classification: LCC KFN5950 .N45 2024 (print) | LCC KFN5950 (ebook) | DDC 347.747/0109034—dc23/eng/20231005
LC record available at https://lccn.loc.gov/2023044355.
LC ebook record available at https://lccn.loc.gov/2023044356.

British Library Cataloguing-in-Publication Data is available.

To judges who understand that law is not simply politics in a different form

Contents

Preface and Acknowledgments

I have dedicated this book to judges who understand that law is not simply politics in a different form. I have long adhered to the judgment that a purely political view of law leads to legal uncertainty and unpredictability, the loss of judicial impartiality, and ultimately social instability. I concede that my judgment, as well as that of late-nineteenth-century New York judges, is a political one. But I have never claimed that law is not influenced by politics, only that law must contain elements beyond politics.

I did not write this book, however, to make a political argument. Rather I sought to test the hypothesis I had advanced in *The Roots of American Bureaucracy* (Cambridge, MA: Harvard University Press, 1982) that late-nineteenth-century judges turned to precedent and Langdellian formalism to avoid political decision-making. Those who read the pages that follow can decide how well that hypothesis is supported.

As always I am indebted to the Filomen D'Agostino and Max E. Greenberg Faculty Research Fund for support. I am indebted to Lillian Barany for excellent research assistance. Stephany Ramos spent hours of work carefully translating an old computer program into the new one used by the University Press of Kansas. I am especially indebted to the members of the NYU Legal

History Colloquium and to the readers for the press for their careful reading of this book in manuscript and their invaluable suggestions for improvement.

Finally, I want to thank my wife, Elaine, and my son, Greg, for their patience while I hide away in my study typing, and my daughter, Leila, and the newest member of the family, my son-in-law, Chris, for their continuing encouragement.

William E. Nelson
Woodmere, NY
July 2023

Introduction

This book is about American judicial conservatism during the closing decades of the nineteenth century and the opening decades of the twentieth. It examines the subject, however, not by studying all jurisdictions but by focusing in detail on the work of judges in a single jurisdiction, New York, together with a glimpse at the work product of U.S. Supreme Court justices. This focus will enable readers to appreciate the totality of judges' work product and the complexity of turn-of-the-century conservatism, rather than obtaining only a partial view gained by examining leading cases, often in the Supreme Court of the United States, the memory of which has been preserved by scholars promoting particular agendas.

In the most important legal history book about the late nineteenth and early twentieth centuries, Morton J. Horwitz describes how "the standard mode of explanation" for "the constitutional history of the *Lochner* era . . . has continued 'to be' premised on a conflict between the 'people' and the 'interests.'" He further describes how "the result has been to buttress historical interpretations that . . . treat the late-nineteenth-century judiciary as having capitulated to big business."[1] One of Horwitz's goals in his book is "to challenge what continues to be the dominant form of legal historiography of the Gilded Age."[2] Accordingly, he does not study the conservatism of the Gilded Age but focuses instead on what he calls "Classical Legal Thought," which he defines as a phenomenon "rooted in . . . an old conservative world view, one that presumed that the existence of decentralized political and economic institutions was the primary reason why America had managed to preserve its freedom."[3]

In the end, however, Horwitz's opus supports the received historiographical wisdom by showing how conservative thinkers deployed classical legal thought to block a redistribution of wealth from the rich to the poor. In analyzing classical legal thought, Horwitz examines "basic dichotomies between state and society, between the market and the family, . . . between politics and the market,"[4] and between law and politics. He argues that "all of these conceptualizations sought to establish a separate, 'natural' realm of non-coercive and non-political transactions free from the dangers of state interference and *redistribution*."[5] "At bottom" classical legal thinkers strove to elaborate a natural and neutral "declaratory theory of the judicial function," under which judges merely found but never made law—a theory that responded to "a long-standing fear of legislative intrusion into the distribution of wealth and privilege."[6]

Horwitz's analysis is subtle and open to competing interpretations. My reading is that Horwitz saw an independent body of classical legal thought developing over the course of the nineteenth century and maturing in the aftermath of the Civil War. But once it had matured, conservative thinkers and judges consciously used it, in Horwitz's language, to capitulate to big business. The received wisdom that conservative judges along with much of the legal profession in the decades between 1860 and 1920 were on the side of big business and the rich thus remains in place.

In another significant but less subtle book, Arnold M. Paul explicitly advances the received wisdom. Paul argues that "the judiciary emerged in the mid-1890's as the principal bulwark of conservative defense," when "American constitutionalism underwent a . . . conservative-oriented revolution which vastly expanded the scope of judicial supremacy."[7] Quoting a late-nineteenth-century lawyer in his concluding chapter, Paul states that "in almost every case" the judiciary expanded its role "in the interest of the rich and powerful and against the rights and interests of the masses of the people."[8] Conservatives did so because they were worried, in Paul's view, about "majority power to effect redistribution" and therefore turned to the judiciary for "protection of property from social upheaval."[9]

Arnold Paul's critique of conservative judging in the late 1800s and early 1900s is not unique. It goes back more than a century. In his paradigm-setting work, *The Supreme Court in United States History*,[10] first published in 1922, Charles Warren did not himself criticize judges for their conservatism. But in several pages of discussion, he reported how others had criticized them for "prejudice in favor of capital" and "for deciding cases in favor of the propertied class."[11]

Recently scholars have begun to question, at least indirectly and obliquely, the received wisdom that turn-of-the-century judges were on the side of big business and the rich. Brian Tamanaha, for one, sees no difference between the reasoning style of turn-of-the-century judges and later New Deal legal realists. His "objective . . . [is] to recover an understanding of judging that has prevailed for well over a century—what . . . [he] call[s] balanced realism," which recognizes that judges "sometimes are influenced by their political and moral views," but at the same time that "practice-related, social, and institutional factors . . . constrain judges, and that judges render generally predictable decisions consistent with the law."[12] Tamanaha's "balanced realism," however, does not explicitly reject the conclusion of Horwitz, Paul, and other progressives that sometimes, at least in some major cases, judges can pursue a policy of supporting big business and the rich. Another scholar, David M. Rabban, likewise does not directly challenge the received view that turn-of-the-century judges practiced "intellectually bankrupt formalism, [as] a way to . . . protect the wealthy while invalidating social legislation in the public interest,"[13] but argues that scholars, mainly in academia, turned to history not for binding precedent in support of pro-business results but to understand processes of legal development and change.[14]

My goal in this book is to challenge directly the received wisdom about turn-of-the-century judges being on the side of big business and the rich. Did New York judges, the primary subjects of this book, routinely decide cases in favor of people who invested capital or who otherwise possessed wealth and against people struggling to earn a living and often surviving in poverty? Progressive legal academics in the early decades of the twentieth century, beginning with Roscoe Pound[15] down to Robert Hale[16] and Felix Frankfurter,[17] criticized the law for results favoring the rich and thereby generated the progressive interpretation of the 1860–1920 period to which later scholars such as Morton Horwitz and Arnold Paul, in large part, have adhered. But is this progressive interpretation correct?

There is evidence to support it. Sometimes judges did uphold results favoring big business and people of wealth. On occasion, as will appear in chapters 4 and 5, judges complained about juries deciding personal injury cases on the basis of sympathy for plaintiffs or prejudice against companies and vested interests. Similarly, as chapter 3 will explain, contract doctrine was restructured from a subjective to an objective theory that facilitated contracting by large, bureaucratic, corporate entities. And the law of agency, which determined the scope of agents' authority by objective standards and permitted agents to act on behalf of undisclosed principals, surely facilitated the operation of large, impersonal corporate entities. Finally, chapter 2 will show how courts recognized a liberty right of businesses not to have unionized employees working in their plants.

These rules typically favoring large businesses were balanced, however, by rules that favored "little fellows"[18]: smaller competitors and other middle-class and poorer individuals. Chapter 6 will report, for example, that some judges explicitly declared that law should be administered to protect the property rights of ordinary people such as homeowners, even if the result was to lower business profits, and that legal doctrines should be structured to prevent the redistribution of wealth from the poor to the rich. Although personal injury law in the mid-nineteenth century contained doctrines of contributory negligence, assumption of risk, and the fellow-servant rule, which often stood in the path of damage recovery by injured plaintiffs, chapter 4 will show that New York judges eroded those doctrines during the half century after 1860 and that the legislature abolished them in the context of workplace injuries in the 1910s. Employers could refuse to employ unionized workers, but, as will appear in chapter 2, courts permitted workers to organize, strike, picket, and effectively shut down many of the employers who would not deal with them. Although corporate law left directors and managers relatively free to run their businesses as they thought best, the law described in chapter 3 also insisted that they act toward many of those with whom they dealt in a fiduciary capacity that required fairness and prohibited fraud. The law of nuisance, discussed in chapter 6, regularly pointed toward decisions in favor of middle-class property owners involved in litigation against large entrepreneurial actors. Finally, chapter 5 will show that New York judges protected the fact-finding power of juries and thereby permitted sympathy rather than pro-business doctrine to enter into the resolution of many cases, the precise number of which cannot be determined.

Thus, New York judges between 1860 and 1920 were not conservative in the sense that they pursued policies consistently favoring the rich. Indeed, many of the accomplishments of the judges were forward-looking and progressive in character. Nonetheless, New York law of the late nineteenth and early twentieth centuries was profoundly conservative in an important, overlapping respect. What overlapped was the judiciary's routine adherence to precedent, an adherence limited only occasionally by a concern to achieve justice in an individual case.

A central question addressed in this book is why New York judges between 1860 and 1920 generally adhered to precedent. I reject the claim sometimes made by legal realists that precedent served as a fictitious veneer for hiding the judges' substantive policy preferences—that is, that judges reasoned backward from the policy results they sought to reach and used precedents as putty in their hands to support their favored results.[19] The difficulty with this claim is that the judges studied in this book had no consistent policy preferences that needed to be hidden by precedent; as readers will see, the decisions of New York judges supported a wide array of interest groups favoring a wide array of policies. The policy to which the judges stated they regularly adhered was to follow precedent. Because they favored no specific substantive policies, we should take them at their word. We should pay attention to the two reasons they identified why precedent was the policy they did support.

The first reason they offered for adhering to precedent was to avoid decisions on the basis of policy choice. The policy they supported was to defend the rule of law and "the law's basic commitments against the encroachments of modern politics."[20] For New York Republicans, the most horrible example of policymaking was Chief Justice Roger Taney's opinion in *Scott v. Sandford*.[21] Abraham Lincoln and other members of his party had made it plain that the chief justice had decided issues of policy in the *Dred Scott* case, that he had thereby behaved politically rather than legally, and that political behavior on the part of judges was wrong. Others had criticized the Supreme Court for political behavior on the part of judges in other cases, in particular the *Legal Tender Cases*,[22] decided by the Chase court.[23] There, the court, after deciding by a 5–3 vote that paper money issued by Congress was not legal tender for the payment of debts, the next year reversed itself and ruled 5–4 after two new appointments by President Ulysses Grant that the paper money was legal tender. In the view of the editors of the *Albany Law Journal*, who anticipated the reversal, this was a "great calamity" contrary to "every consideration of prudence, propriety and dignity."[24]

New York lawyers and judges also objected to political judging that was occurring on the local level. Although Fernando Wood, a leader of Tammany Hall, remarked in the late 1860s that "judges were often called on to decide on political questions, and he was sorry to say the majority of them decided according to their political bias" and that he therefore found it "absolutely necessary to look to ... [a] candidate's political principles" in deciding whom to "nominate to the bench,"[25] many New York lawyers and judges disagreed.

The negative consequences of Wood's appointment practices emerged in 1868 and 1869 cases involving the New York Central's unsuccessful effort to take over the Erie Railroad and the Erie's subsequent effort to take over the Albany and Susquehanna. The Erie ultimately formed an alliance with Tammany Hall that gave it access to two judges with a reputation as slaves of the ring, who in fact decided every matter brought before them by the railroad's lawyers in favor of the Erie, including the grant of injunctions having statewide effect. The Erie's opponents, in turn, went to upstate judges, who enjoined the downstate injunctions. What resulted was "a conflict between the judiciary of New York City and that of the country," as "the system of electing judges by the popular vote ... brought forth bitter fruit, and men ... elevated to the bench who should have ornamented the dock." Conflict could have been avoided only by "judicial respect for judicial action; courtesy and confidence were the essence of it," but "these had ... long passed away." The contests between the Erie Railroad and its opponents became "altogether too ludicrous" and brought "the courts and the laws of New York into ridicule and contempt."[26] One New York lawyer who particularly recoiled from the Erie scandal was Christopher Columbus Langdell, who left New York practice to become Dane Professor and dean at Harvard Law School, where he perfected his precedent-based approach to legal analysis.[27]

Out of concern for the law's "expos[ure] ... to partisan influences,"[28] New York lawyers accordingly organized the Association of the Bar of the City of New York in 1870 and played a leadership role in organizing the American Bar Association in 1878.[29] Their goal in the founding of both was to remove law from politics by denying judges the power to make policy judgments. Resolution of disputes through the application of preexisting law was a ready alternative to deciding issues of political and social policy and thereby making new law as the Taney and Chase courts had done. Until the end of the nineteenth century, New York's lawyers and judges all appreciated the necessity of avoiding the cataclysmic social and political conflict of the sort that had led to the Civil War and to corruption in its aftermath.[30]

The lawyers produced voluminous writing on the subject of stare decisis, or adherence to precedent. Thus, the editors of the *Albany Law Journal* wrote in 1872 that without stare decisis there could be "no security of property" either for ordinary citizens or the wealthy and "no stable or consistent administration of justice."[31] Another New York lawyer, quoting the great New York jurist James Kent, elaborated upon this point. He wrote:

> It would be ... extremely inconvenient to the public, if precedent were not duly regarded and ... followed. It is by the notoriety and stability of such rules that ... people in general can venture with confidence to buy and trust, and to deal with each other. If judicial decisions were to be lightly

disregarded, we should disturb and unsettle the great land-
marks of property.[32]

And an 1880 article explained a second point:

> Courts are frequently called upon to decide questions in
> which not individuals merely, but the whole people, take
> an interest, and in regard to which prejudices have become
> excited and passions inflamed. There must be an arbiter
> somewhere, to decide such questions, which will command
> respect, or they will be brought to the arbitrament of force;
> and nothing will contribute so much to secure this respect
> as a steady uniformity of decision. . . . The overthrow of a
> single decision in a case of that character, unless upon rea-
> sons so clear and conclusive as scarcely to admit of contro-
> versy, is seriously to be deprecated, as tending to perpetuate
> an existing conflict of opinion.[33]

The twenty-three-year-old *Dred Scott* decision clearly remained
in this writer's consciousness.

Significant attention was paid to the work of these writers
by the court of appeals, which is New York's highest court with
appellate jurisdiction over the Supreme Courts, which are the
states' primary trial courts.[34] In a leading 1892 case, for instance,
the court of appeals took up the question of how judges should
address issues of policy when they had to decide them. The court
noted that it was "not always easy to determine . . . public policy"
and that "judges [in] . . . act[ing] upon what they have deemed
sound public policy" had sometimes "undoubtedly, in some measure, and in a remote sense, assumed legislative functions."[35] The
court condemned such judging. Recognizing that it was "difficult
to define and limit the power thus to enforce public policy which
is not found in the statute law," the court nonetheless held that
the power "should be exercised only in clear cases, and gener-

ally within limits already defined by decisions of acknowledged authority." It saw "no occasion for stretching the power so as to apply it to new or doubtful cases in a state where the legislature is in session one-third of the year, and thus competent to indicate the public will."[36] When it was "deemed wise to extend" public policy, "the lawmaking power, and not the courts, should do it,"[37] which is exactly what, as chapter 4 will show, New York did in the context of negligence law. Quoting Justice Joseph Story, the opinion concluded that judges were "not at liberty to look at general considerations of the supposed public interests and policy" of the state "beyond what its constitution and laws and judicial decisions make known to us." Any inquiry into policy "beyond these limits, will be found to be one of great vagueness and uncertainty, and to involve discussions which scarcely come within the range of judicial duty and functions, and upon which men may and will complexionally differ."[38]

The court of appeals took the same position in numerous other cases. It ruled that judges were "not to consider the question as one simply of sound or of good policy, but whether there is any known public policy."[39] Although the "term 'public policy' [was] frequently used in a very vague, loose, or inaccurate sense," the court ruled that the "state can have no public policy except what is to be found in its ... constitution, ... statutes, or judicial records."[40] The "policy of the state [was] to be determined by its positive laws, or in cases concerning matters upon which they are silent by the decisions of its courts"[41] as "sanctioned by the common law and expounded by the ablest jurists."[42]

The cases required, in sum, that judges "adhere to the plain language of the law" rather than "resort to the unsafe ground of ... public policy"[43] and led to decisions such as the one in *O'Connor v. Hendrick*[44] upholding a rule, which was adopted by the state superintendent of public instruction pursuant to language in the state constitution prohibiting sectarian influences in public schools, that barred teachers in public schools from wearing religious garb in the classroom. Some readers may disagree with the result in the *O'Connor* case, but the case makes my main point clearly: that judges were to follow policies enacted into written law or adopted through past lines of common-law precedent and thereby avoid evaluating the wisdom or justice of those policies. The job of judges was to resolve disputes under existing law, not to use those disputes as an opportunity to select social policies that would make new law. Only in the absence of enacted law or past precedent were judges free to make policy, but even then their duty was not to make policy choices but to frame the law, as chapter 2 will show they did in the context of employer-employee rights, on the basis of widely shared social values such as the free-labor ideology of the Civil War and antebellum periods.

The second reason given by lawyers and judges for adhering to precedent or following law enacted in the past was a faith on their part that old law was better than new law, a faith that the values of the early republic to which they were prepared to turn, whatever those values were, were more noble and better than the profit-centered values of the late nineteenth century. The legal profession, that is, believed that it should serve "as guardian of the nation's most fundamental values."[45] Key members of the profession were "nostalgic for the values of individualism, independence, and equality ... prevalent before the Civil War" and stressed the need to revive "the theory and practice of the early republic."[46] Fidelity to precedent under this second view was thus about preserving the ongoing character of the law inherited from the nation's founding.

In preserving old values, judges continued to apply, as chapter 7 will show, traditional Christian religious and sexual norms—norms that we can assume the judges believed were morally good. They also applied nuisance law, which is discussed in chapter 6, that protected established property rights and preexisting land uses. Perhaps the most important conservative response of New

York judges occurred when, as shown in chapter 5, the legislature abolished common law pleading and merged law and equity, but the courts applied the legislation in a narrow fashion and thereby preserved both the common law and the fact-finding discretion of juries.

The innovations sanctioned by the judiciary were few and unavoidable. As business enterprises grew and exerted increasing power over the community, judges elaborated three bodies of doctrine. One, as described in chapter 1, was the upholding of most regulatory statutes enacted by the legislature. A second, which is discussed in chapter 3, was to empower managers and directors instead of owners to administer businesses, but subject to a body of fiduciary law constraining them to deal fairly and without fraud. A third, also discussed in chapter 3, was a move from a subjective to an objective theory of contract and agency law.

On the whole, however, New York's judges continued to apply and administer old, established law. Arguably they did so, as suggested above, because they thought that established law was good law and that applying old law would support and promote a good society. As one New York congressman declared in an 1876 speech to the House of Representatives, it was necessary to "bring back that better era of the republic in which, when men consecrated themselves to public service, they utterly abnegated all selfish purposes."[47] Many others, including leading members of the New York bar, agreed that the early leaders of the nation had enacted law in pursuit of the public interest as a whole, not in pursuit of narrow special interests.[48] They saw old law as good law and turned to it to "revive a past renown" and "give new life to traditions which . . . [were] only dormant, not extinct."[49] When they looked backward to the legal system of a hundred years earlier, lawyers, judges, and scholars of the late nineteenth century saw founding fathers such as John Adams, who believed that "every possible Case . . . [should be] settled in a Precedent"[50] and sought in the Massachusetts Constitution of 1780 to establish "a government of laws and not of men,"[51] and John Marshall, who promised in *Marbury v. Madison*[52] to remove the Supreme Court from politics and decide only questions of law.[53] Thinkers of the late nineteenth century thought, with good reason but ultimately wrongly, that lawyers and judges of an earlier time had behaved apolitically and had consistently bound themselves to preexisting rules of law.

Unfortunately, New York judges rarely articulated the two reasons just discussed for following precedent. Consistent with their effort to be apolitical, they simply adhered to precedent. Accordingly, the chapters that follow will be unable to distinguish the cases in which judges applied precedent so as to avoid policymaking from those in which they followed old law because they thought it to be good law. Thus, the chapters that follow and that discuss New York case law can establish only three basic points. First, they will show that New York judges did not favor big business and the rich but instead laid the foundation for the liberalism of future governors Alfred E. Smith, Franklin D, Roosevelt, and Herbert Lehman. Second, the chapters will show that courts did modify the law when developing economic conditions compelled them to do so. But third, judges followed precedent and applied old law whenever they could.

Part One

Judicial Support for Both "Little Fellows" and the Rich

I

Judicial Deference to Progressive Legislation

Police Power and Regulation

Lochner v. New York[1] was surely the most infamous case during
the entire six-decade period between 1860 and 1920. In *Lochner*, decided in 1905, the Supreme Court of the United States
invalidated a New York statute that limited to sixty the number of hours per week that men in the bakery industry could
work. What is noteworthy, however, is that the Supreme Court
reversed the New York Court of Appeals, which had taken a
"broad-minded view" that the constitution could change to "conform to the wishes of the citizens as they may deem best for the
public welfare" and had thereby upheld the statute.[2] The constitution, according to the New York court, had been "made for
an undefined and expanding future" in which "new and various
experiences . . . [would] mould and shape it into new and not less
useful forms."[3] The New York court had no doubt that "the natural right to life, liberty and the pursuit of happiness [was] not
an absolute right . . . [but] must yield whenever the concession is
demanded by the welfare, health or prosperity of the state. The
individual must sacrifice his particular interest or desires if the

sacrifice is a necessary one in order that organized society as a whole shall be benefited."[4]

The New York courts, of course, had recorded their own infamous cases invalidating legislative regulations on constitutional grounds. The most notorious such case was *Matter of Jacobs*,[5] decided in 1885. At issue was a statute prohibiting the manufacture of cigars or processing of tobacco on any floor on which any person resided in any tenement in New York City or Brooklyn housing four or more families. The court could not make sense of the law and concluded:

> This law was not intended to protect the health of those engaged in cigarmaking, as they are allowed to manufacture cigars everywhere except in the forbidden tenement-houses. It cannot be perceived how the cigarmaker is to be improved in his health or his morals by forcing him from his home and its hallowed associations and beneficent influences, to ply his trade elsewhere. It was not intended to protect the health of that portion of the public not residing in the forbidden tenement-houses, as cigars are allowed to be manufactured in private houses, [or] in large factories and shops. . . . Nor was it intended to improve or protect the health of the occupants of tenement-houses. If there are but three families in the tenement-house, however numerous and gregarious their members may be, the manufacture is not forbidden. . . . It is plain that . . . it has no relation whatever to the public health.[6]

The statute was therefore unconstitutional. Infamous as the *Jacobs* case may be, it must be noted that its holding protected the entrepreneurial opportunities of "little fellows" in the cigar-making industry,[7] not big cigar-making businesses or the rich.

Yet another notorious court of appeals decision was *Ives v. South Buffalo Ry. Co.*,[8] which in 1911 declared New York's newly enacted workers' compensation law unconstitutional. But this result endured for only a few years. In 1913, New York's voters approved a constitutional amendment authorizing the legislature to enact a new workers' compensation law,[9] and the legislature promptly did so.[10] In 1915, the court of appeals upheld the constitutionality of that law in *Jensen v. Southern Pacific Co.*[11]

The most frequent occasions on which New York courts ruled statutes unconstitutional involved regulations "which, by discrimination or otherwise, prevent[ed] an individual's pursuing a lawful vocation."[12] Among the statutes invalidated were one prohibiting the manufacture or sale of oleomargarine,[13] one prohibiting the employment of aliens by contractors engaged in constructing public works,[14] one prohibiting the sale of preservatives for use in butter and cheese,[15] one prohibiting the boiling of garbage or offal in New York City or treating either with steam,[16] one requiring licensing of horseshoers,[17] one requiring licensing of dancing academies in New York City,[18] one requiring anyone seeking to be licensed as an undertaker also to be licensed as an embalmer,[19] one requiring anyone selling insurance policies to affirm that he was engaged principally in the insurance business or as a real estate agent,[20] one prohibiting distribution of advertising matter on city streets,[21] one prohibiting the use in public buildings of stone quarried out of state,[22] and one prohibiting shipment of milk within the state except by a person or entity transacting business at an office in the state.[23]

Another line of cases invalidated legislation prohibiting the sale of tickets by individuals who were not employees of the common carrier or other entity that would redeem the ticket.[24] Retroactive legislation was sometimes struck down.[25] Other cases dealt with the licensing of dogs[26] and the killing of dangerous ones,[27] the taking down of dangerous buildings,[28] closing a reservoir and replacing it with a park,[29] prohibiting construction of buildings within thirty feet of a parkway,[30] prohibiting the use of the United States or state flag in advertising,[31] prohibiting private bankers from receiving deposits averaging less than $500 unless they received a license,[32] prohibiting the taking of ice from lakes and ponds used as a source of water supply,[33] offering real property for sale without written authority of the owner,[34] making it unlawful for a food merchant to give gifts tied to the purchase of food,[35] and making the sale of inventory and fixtures of a business in bulk fraudulent as against creditors.[36] Other cases that struck down regulations dealt with railroads and utilities in connection with such matters as rate setting,[37] demands for free or reduced-rate service,[38] the use of streets and obligations to repair and maintain them,[39] and the disposition of assets upon bankruptcy and corporate dissolution.[40]

The cases holding legislative acts unconstitutional that have just been discussed constituted only a small minority, however, of New York's constitutional cases between 1860 and 1920. The New York courts during those six decades did not have a narrow view of legislative power; on the contrary, they read the most significant head of power—the police power—quite broadly. The result of their reading is that the courts in the aftermath of the Civil War and the opening decades of the twentieth century progressively laid the foundation for the modern regulatory state of the mid- and late twentieth century.

A unanimous 1905 opinion by the Court of Appeals set the standard. It declared:

> If the statute comes fairly within the scope of the police power it is a valid law, although it may interfere, in some respects, with the liberty of the citizen. . . . A statute to promote the public health, the public safety or to secure public order or for the prevention or suppression of fraud is a valid law. . . . All business and occupations are conducted subject to the exercise of the police power. . . . *It may be laid down as a general principle that legislation is valid which has for its object the promotion of the public health, safety, morals, conve-*

*nience and general welfare or the prevention of fraud or immo-
rality.*[41]

A lower court added that it could "not attempt to limit or restrain
the exercise of legislative authority within its appointed sphere."
The court found it within the province of the legislature "to deal
with every element of human experience involved in the life of
the community or of any class thereof" and "with any condition,
general or special, however manifested or brought to the knowledge of the law-making power."[42]

These same values were expressed in one of the court of appeal's earliest cases after 1860, *Metropolitan Bank v. Van Dyck.*[43]
In *Metropolitan Bank*, the court in 1863 upheld congressional legislation that made paper money issued to fund the Civil War
legal tender for the payment of all debts, public and private. The
court must have been influenced by the fact that the legislation
was that of Congress, not the state legislature, and that it had
been enacted in the midst of the Civil War. It declared that it
could not give the law "such a construction as will cripple the
government, and render it unequal to the objects for which it was
instituted."[44] Although *Metropolitan Bank* was not a police power
case, the court treated congressional power as an equivalent of
police power; the court understood that it was being asked "to
annul" a law "passed . . . after grave deliberation by both houses
of Congress . . . with the approval of the executive."[45]

Accordingly, it quoted Justice Story at length:

Every form of government unavoidably includes a grant
of some discretionary powers. It would be wholly imbecile
without them. It is impossible to foresee all the exigencies
which may arise in the progress of events. . . . There must be
left to those who administer the government a large mass
of discretionary powers capable of greater or less actual ex-
pansion, according to circumstances, and sufficiently flexible

not to involve the nation in utter destruction from the rigid
limitations imposed upon it by an improvident jealousy.
Every power, however limited, as well as broad, is in its
own nature susceptible of abuse. No Constitution can provide perfect guards against it. Confidence must be reposed
somewhere; and in free governments, the ordinary securities
against abuse are found in the responsibility of rulers to the
people, and in the just exercise of the elective franchise, and
ultimately in the sovereign power of change belonging to
them.[46]

Another key case arising out of the Civil War that was not specifically a police powers case was *Darlington v. Mayor of City of New
York*,[47] which similarly displayed judicial deference by upholding
legislation adopted in 1855,[48] the effect of which was to require
the city to compensate property owners whose property had been
damaged during the 1863 draft riots.

Early police power cases took a similar approach of deference
to the political process. These early cases typically involved the
closing down of inappropriate businesses in densely populated
districts. Several such cases occurred in the 1860s. An 1867 case,
for instance, involved the manufacture of lime from seashells at
a factory on East Fifteenth Street in lower Manhattan,[49] and an
1868 case involved a slaughterhouse on Fourth Street near what
is now New York University and Washington Square Park.[50] Another 1868 case upheld the power of the captain of the port of
New York to set aside certain piers for use by canal boats during
specified times of year.[51]

A wide variety of cases quickly occurred. An 1871 case upheld
legislation authorizing the seizure of animals running at large in
public highways,[52] and an 1875 case approved legislation prohibiting possession of specified game birds in an effort to conserve
their species.[53] Two important cases were decided in 1878. The
first upheld a criminal conviction for bringing adulterated milk

into New York City.[54] The second affirmed a damage judgment authorized by a statute in favor of a plaintiff injured by an intoxicated person against an owner of property who knew that intoxicating liquors were to be served on his or her premises.[55]

A similarly broad range of cases was decided in the 1880s. Regulation of insurance companies was upheld as early as 1880.[56] An important case distinguished *People v. Marks*,[57] which had invalidated legislation prohibiting the manufacture or sale of oleomargarine, and upheld the constitutionality of a statute that prohibited the addition of artificial yellow coloring to the oleomargarine to make it look like butter.[58] Another upheld legislation for placing local railways propelled by electricity underground.[59] A striking case in 1888 affirmed the conviction of an owner of a skating rink who refused to sell entrance tickets to three African American men in violation of state legislation prohibiting the exclusion of people from theaters or other places of amusement on account of race or previous condition of servitude. The state statute was upheld despite the argument of the defense counsel that the "legislature [was] not omnipotent" and that the police power did not give it authority to "establish social relations" or "promote[] amalgamation," with the court noting that "members of the African race . . . are citizens." The court accordingly made a moral judgment, pursuant to the police power, that "justice and the public interest concur in a policy which shall elevate them [i.e., African Americans] as individuals and relieve them from oppressive or degrading discrimination, . . . and give them a fair chance in the struggle of life."[60]

The court of appeals' broad reading of the police power persisted in the 1890s. In one 1891 case, it ruled that the police power gave a city the authority to order a telegraph company to remove its aboveground poles and wires adjacent to streets and place its wires underground,[61] and in another it affirmed the power of municipalities to prohibit burials within their boundaries.[62] In 1892, it sustained legislation allowing the Long Island Railroad to power its trains running along Atlantic Avenue in Brooklyn with steam,[63] and in 1895 it upheld legislation requiring the licensing of plumbers, declaring that "the drainage and sewerage, whether of public works and buildings, or of private tenements, [should] be as skillfully planned and carried out, as the modern standard of science admits" and that "the work of plumbing . . . is generally recognized to be essential to comfort and health" and "should be the subject of some supervision by the authorities."[64] In 1898, the appellate division approved a legislative grant to municipalities to compel the use of correct weights and measures.[65]

Perhaps the most important regulatory cases occurred in the years around the turn of the century. The earliest case was *Health Department of City of New York v. Rector of Trinity Church*.[66] In 1887, the legislature had enacted that every tenement house erected or converted after 1867 had to be supplied with sufficient quantities of public reservoir water on every floor occupied by one or more families.[67] The church objected that to retrofit its buildings with water would entail great expense. But, in an opinion by Judge Rufus Peckham, the court of appeals responded that, although "we may own our property absolutely," "it is subject to the proper exercise of the police power. . . . It must be so used as not improperly to cause harm to our neighbor. . . . There are sometimes necessary expenses . . . which we must incur . . . in order that the general health, safety or welfare may be conserved."[68] Nine years later in the *Moeschen* case,[69] the court upheld a provision of the Tenement House Act of 1901 requiring the replacement of school sinks,[70] which sanitary inspectors often found were not "flushed for weeks" and were "a serious menace to the health of the occupants of tenements, with proper water-closet accommodations," each in separate rooms at the rate of one bathroom for every two families in the tenement. Although the defendant argued that the replacement of school sinks with water closets would involve an expense that "would practically destroy" her equity in the building, the court of appeals unanimously upheld that 1901 act.[71] Following the Triangle Shirtwaist Factory fire in 1911, the courts went on to uphold rules requiring the installation of fire escapes,[72] automatic sprinklers in factory buildings,[73] and fire-proof elevators.[74]

In the decade and a half after *Moeschen*, the court of appeals decided two other major cases that would produce a vast amount of regulatory activity and litigation in the decades to come. One of them, noted earlier in this chapter, was *Jensen v. Southern Pacific Co.*,[75] which upheld the constitutionality of the workers' compensation law. The other was *Lincoln Trust Co. v. Williams Building Corp.*,[76] which affirmed the constitutionality of municipal zoning. In the time between *Moeschen* and *Lincoln Trust*, New York courts also upheld a wide variety of other police power legislation, including a requirement that physicians sign death certificates,[77] the licensing of butchers,[78] the exclusion of unvaccinated children from public schools,[79] the regulation of employment agencies,[80] the regulation of removal of mineral water from mineral springs,[81] the prohibition of violation of trademarks,[82] the regulation of transmission of money to foreign countries,[83] the regulation of insurance companies and insurance agents,[84] the regulation of storage of gasoline,[85] the regulation of sewer construction,[86] the regulation of garbage collection,[87] the education and licensing of dentists,[88] the regulation of banking,[89] the licensing of hackmen,[90] the registration of pharmacies,[91] the regulation of shipment of calf carcasses,[92] and the false representation of ordinary meat as kosher.[93] The New York courts, it appears, were willing to sustain regulatory initiatives of almost any sort as they lay the foundations of the modern regulatory state.

A key subject for the courts was regulation of rates charged by railroads, utilities, and other businesses affected with a public interest. Judges understood rate-setting to be a legislative function, albeit one that the legislature could delegate to an administrative agency.[94] But a regulated entity could appeal to the courts if the regulated rate was set so low that it would deprive its shareholders of a reasonable profit upon the actual value of the plant and property of the entity.[95] For the most part, New York courts sustained the rate-setting authority of the legislature[96] and subordinate administrative agencies.[97] They also sustained legislation to facilitate the construction of railroads[98] and street railways[99] and the lighting of towns by gas lamps[100] and orders about the free placement of gas meters,[101] the placement and operation of gates at railroad crossings,[102] the building of freight stations,[103] the repair of streets along routes used by railroads,[104] the approval of railroad routes,[105] and the termination or corporate reorganization of railroads.[106]

New York courts also upheld other legislation not grounded in the police power. As the court of appeals declared in upholding a statute prohibiting the use of a living person's name or picture without permission, "the power of the legislature in the absence of any constitutional restriction to declare that a particular act shall constitute a crime or be actionable as a tort cannot be questioned."[107] In light of this declaration, courts upheld anti-monopoly legislation,[108] the reorganization of municipal governments[109] and of the New York City police department,[110] the power of state judges to call out the National Guard to suppress riots,[111] the power of boards of education to reduce teachers' salaries,[112] the repeal of legislation authorizing suits against municipalities for negligently maintained streets,[113] and retroactive laws expanding creditors' rights in connection with legal arrangements made before enactment of the laws.[114] Legislative power to regulate and otherwise make law was vast indeed.

Eminent Domain

Distantly related to regulation and the police power was the law of eminent domain. If a court concluded that a police power regulation was unconstitutional and therefore void, government might nonetheless be able to achieve its regulatory goals by taking title to the property it had sought to regulate and paying just compensation to its owner. To understand how the law of eminent domain fit with regulatory law, it is necessary to address two sets of issues: (1) what was the scope of the government's power to condemn property, and (2) what was the just measure of damages.

SCOPE OF EMINENT DOMAIN POWER

Both the federal and state constitutions permitted the taking of private property only for public use.[115] Nevertheless, for the most part, judges behaved with considerable deference and allowed state and municipal governments to take property whenever and for whatever reason they wanted. Judges upheld, for example, the delegation of eminent domain power to private entities such as railroads,[116] ferries,[117] electric companies,[118] gas companies,[119] water companies,[120] and cemeteries that did not exclude any person from being buried on equal terms with other persons.[121] They also upheld the use of eminent domain power to preserve the beauty of the Hudson River Palisades[122] and to obtain land to extend Central Park[123] and to build a road to serve three farms.[124] After much doubt and debate about whether eminent domain could be used to facilitate the drainage of one person's swamp land over the land of another,[125] the legislature enacted a statute permitting such drainage,[126] and the courts sustained its constitutionality.[127] But a private entity could use eminent domain power only for the specific purpose for which the power had been granted and for no other purpose, albeit a public one.[128] The state court of claims also ruled that use of a farm by National Guard soldiers constituted a trespass and not an eminent domain taking,[129] and the New York City Court of Common Pleas held that an entry into an apartment to extinguish a fire that did not in fact exist likewise constituted a trespass requiring compensation in damages.[130]

Just Compensation

A progressive seeking to redistribute wealth from those who possessed it to those who were less fortunate would want to limit the damages paid when the power of eminent domain was exercised; limiting damages would keep wealth in the hands of the public and out of the hands of rich private property owners. Essentially there were two ways to achieve this result. The one was to hold that whatever wealth was taken was not property and thus did not require compensation. The other was to sustain jury verdicts awarding low judgments and to reverse verdicts giving high awards. The cases do not provide sufficient evidence to know for certain whether progressives achieved their aim, but they suggest that the progressives failed.

On the issue whether things of value constituted property, the courts tended not to be progressive. The court of appeals consistently held, for example, that owners of property abutting on city streets possessed easements in those streets giving them a right to ingress and egress from their property and that any significant interference with that right entitled the owners to just compensation.[131] New York courts also held that a railroad's contractual right to run its trains on the tracks of another railroad constituted property for which just compensation had to be paid,[132] that oyster beds planted under public waters constituted compensable property when they were destroyed by sewage,[133] and that the right to the flow of water in a stream was property.[134] Of course, when New York City took land to enhance its water supply, just compensation was required.[135] But the court of appeals also held that a judgment lien on property was not itself property, and thus the lienor did not need to be compensated if the property was condemned.[136]

As to damages, courts in general upheld generous awards,[137] including interest,[138] but in the absence of evidence of significant damage, they could direct a verdict for nominal damages only.[139] Of course, damages could be paid by an assessment on property owners who benefitted from a project,[140] and property owners who gained a benefit from an improvement would have the value of that benefit deducted from any damages due them.[141] Unlike the cases dealing with the police power and regulation, none of the cases just discussed establish that New York's courts consistently took a deferential, progressive approach toward eminent domain. Instead, their approach was a mixed one. They obeyed the law and granted government broad power to engage in public projects but took the requirement of just compensation seriously.

Taxation

New York's courts, in contrast, were totally deferential to the legislature on the subject of taxation, thereby leaving the legislature free to use taxes to redistribute wealth from the rich to the poor. As the court of appeals declared, "the power of the state legislature to impose taxes is unlimited . . . guided and restrained [only] by . . . considerations of wisdom and of policy."[142] The court later noted that "the power of taxation . . . inherent in the people . . . is vested in the legislature . . . , and, except as restrained by the Federal Constitution, its exercise for public purposes is unlimited."[143] On the basis of statements such as these, the courts upheld a tax on out-of-state fire insurance companies doing business in New York,[144] a stock transfer tax,[145] a mortgage tax,[146] a tax on property transferred at death by deed,[147] a franchise tax imposed on corporations for the privilege of doing business,[148] and local improvement assessments on properties benefitting from an improvement.[149] "An honest effort" had to "be made to place the burden of taxation so that it will rest equally upon all property according to fair valuations,"[150] but courts nonetheless sustained many legislative exemptions from taxes for charities such as hospitals,[151] for trust companies,[152] for personal property of fire insurance companies,[153] and for railroads in rural localities that did not need to be assessed for the protection of highways crossing railroad tracks.[154] Occasional taxes, such as an amendment to the manner of assessing the stock transfer tax, were invalidated on grounds of inequality,[155] as was a tax on remainders and reversions vesting prior to June 30, 1885, on the ground that it discriminated against a limited class of remaindermen.[156]

Summary

New York law dealing with regulation, eminent domain, and taxation surely did not consistently favor big business or people of wealth. Far more often than not, New York courts upheld the regulation of business, thereby increasing the costs of doing business and reducing profits. In particular, New York judges upheld regulations, such as the Tenement House Act of 1901, which increased the well-being of some of New York City's poorest residents at significant expense to their landlords, and the workers' compensation law of 1914, which guaranteed remedies to injured workers at significant expense to their employers. Even in *Matter of Jacobs*, one of the most infamous cases that invalidated regulation, the court of appeals appeared to side with individual workers striving to maintain their independence against organized firms seeking to control those workers by turning them into employees. While New York courts appear to have required full compensation for property taken by eminent domain, the judges did give the state broad freedom to take land that it wanted. They also gave the legislature extensive freedom to redistribute wealth through taxation.

Of course, there were some pro-business decisions, and those decisions meant that, although the courts were not conservative in the sense of consistently favoring business and the rich, neither were they consistently progressive in the sense of facilitating social change in the interests of the poor. Judges were doing something different in the context of regulation, eminent domain, and taxation. They were, in large part, following precedent and applying the law of their predecessors. They were not changing the law. In this sense, they were conservative. But they were yielding to the legislature enormous freedom to redistribute wealth and power and thereby to change society. In this sense, they were quite progressive, but in the conservative fashion that American courts had always been progressive throughout the antebellum era of the nineteenth century.

2

Labor Law

On the subject of labor law like regulatory, eminent domain, and taxation law, New York judges made both conservative and progressive contributions during the decades between 1860 and 1920. Judges recognized that they were dealing with "interesting and perplexing" questions that "involve[d] legal and sociological problems of the highest importance," questions that lay "at the very foundations of the relations between employer and employee." They understood that their decisions would "interfere, more or less, with individual freedom of action."[1]

The Right to Organize, Strike, and Picket

The most important body of progressive doctrine gave workers the right to organize, the right to strike, and the right to picket peacefully. In the 1891 case of *Rogers v. Evarts*,[2] for example, the state's supreme court declared:

> The tendency of modern thought and judicial decision is to the enlargement of the right of combination. . . . Irrespec-

tive of any statute, . . . the law now permits workmen . . . to combine together, and by peaceable means to seek any legitimate advantage in their trade. The increase of wages is such an advantage. The right to combine involves of necessity the right to persuade all co-laborers to join in the combination.[3]

The court of appeals went even further. It upheld a contract between employers and unions permitting the employment by an employer only of union members, which it looked upon as "an agreement voluntarily made by an employer with his workmen"—as "a private agreement between an employer and his employees." The court added that for a union "to coerce workmen to become members of the employees' organization" was not something "necessarily . . . contravening public policy."[4] The court also upheld the right of union workers to boycott the use by their employer of raw materials or other supplies produced by nonunion workers.[5] Finally, the court upheld the right of a union to refuse to work with members of a rival union and to go on strike to enforce its refusal. In so holding, it reiterated the basic principle:

It is not the duty of one man to work for another unless he has agreed to, and . . . either may end the contract whenever he chooses. The one may work, or refuse to work, at will, and the other may hire or discharge at will. The terms of employment are subject to mutual agreement. . . . Whatever one man may do alone, he may do in combination with others.[6]

In short, the basic principle of free labor that had produced the abolition of slavery half a century earlier was simply being reiterated, albeit with the addition that people could do in combination whatever they were permitted to do alone.

The court of appeals did, however, hold unconstitutional legislation that prohibited employers from firing workers who joined
unions.[7] The court explained that the same "freedom to contract
which entitles an employer to make by agreement his place of
business wholly within the control of a labor union" also "entitles
him, if he so desires, to require of his employees that they be
wholly independent of any labor union."[8] The main difference
between the turn-of-the-century law of the New York Court of
Appeals and the law three-and-a-half decades later under the
Wagner Act[9] thus was not hostility on the part of the court of
appeals to the interests of labor. The court gave labor significant
rights, but it insisted that unions exploit those rights not at the
legislative or administrative level but on the ground through the
resolution of particular conflicts between union locals and individual business entities. The law was centrally about parties
freely arriving at the contracts they desired. Of course, employers
typically had greater bargaining power than employees, but the
court did what it could to equalize that power by upholding the
right of workers to organize and bargain collectively and thereby
make freedom of contract more just.

Lower courts adhered to these rules. The appellate division,
for instance, upheld the right of members of trade unions to refuse to work with anyone who did not belong to their union,[10]
and a trial judge upheld the right of a union to strike for higher
pay. The same judge also upheld the right of members of the
union to support their fellow members by striking against another company and of union members from both firms to picket
peacefully.[11] Another trial judge upheld the right of employers to
form an organization to seek agreements with unionized workers
to resolve disputes through arbitration rather than work stop-
pages.[12]

But, although New York judges gave both management and
workers vast leeway to reach almost any agreements they wished,

the judges did set limits on what unions were permitted to do. "Labor unions" were "recognized by the courts ... as a legitimate and useful part of the industrial system ... and protected by the law of this state." But they were not permitted to "injure the property rights of another by the means of causing or controlling through duress, coercion, oppression or fraud, the acts of third persons which produce[d] injury." Thus, the court of appeals upheld an injunction against the labor unions of Auburn, New York, when they combined to induce businesses in town to cease patronizing an employer who refused to compel its employees to join a union the employees did not wish to join.[13] The appellate division agreed that striking employees could not "attempt to prevent employment of others" to replace them "as a means to better success in the strike ... , if efforts of a coercive character amounting to more than peaceable persuasion were invoked." "Intimidation," "assault," and "violence" were forbidden.[14] The law," one trial judge noted, was "settled." Strikers could,

> by picketing, attempt to peaceably persuade other work-
> men not to enter his [the employer's] employment and
> take their vacant places, and even to persuade their former
> fellow workmen still remaining in the service, to leave and
> join them in the strike. Their efforts to attain such result,
> however, must be confined to acts of peaceable persuasion.
> Certainly they may not extend to violence, threats, or even
> verbal abuse; and, if they do so extend, they thereby become
> unlawful.[15]

The difficulty with this settled law was drawing the boundary between peaceable persuasion, on the one hand, and violence, threats, and verbal abuse, on the other. Were pickets standing immediately adjacent to each other in front of a factory entrance threatening? If someone seeking to enter the factory pushed one of them aside to get by and the picket who was pushed shoved back in return, was that violence? If a picketer reminded someone who continued to work of the criminal record of that worker's father, was that verbal abuse? These were all issues of fact that trial judges needed to decide, and the discretion to decide those issues gave the judges vast power to determine the legality or illegality of strikes. As a trial judge observed in one case, "when it is sought to draw a line between what is permissible and what is forbidden, it is difficult to say logically why a certain act should be placed on the one side or the other. The courts must be governed in their action by common sense and considerations of public policy."[16] As another judge wrote, "The whole question turn[ed] . . . upon the purpose for which the act [was] done." Acts done "for the purpose of injuring" a "business or its good will were illegal"; those done for "procuring employment for their fellow members who work in mills," or for "procuring a market for such work" were permissible.[17]

The reported cases suggest a conservative, pro-business leaning on the part of most trial judges. In *Heitkamper v. Hoffmann*,[18] for example, the court described how various union members or supporters, usually numbering six to ten men, would periodically march up and down the street in front of Heitkamper's bakery. They sometimes wore placards advising the public not to buy bread from Heitkamper but to buy it from a baker across the street who conducted a union shop. At times, the picketers blocked entrance to Heitkamper's bakery, spit on the sidewalk, and "made faces" at employees in the store. On the basis of these facts, the court concluded that "the plaintiff's business ha[d] been injured, his receipts ha[d] materially fallen off, and he ha[d] suffered many annoyances and much inconvenience. A continuance of these acts [would], no doubt, result in financial disaster to the plaintiff," who therefore sought and to whom the court granted injunctive relief.[19]

Michaels v. Hillman[20] was similar. It was a major case, in which

Sidney Hillman, the president of the Amalgamated Clothing Workers of America, was represented by Emory Buckner and Felix Frankfurter, among others. The case

> turn[ed] upon the question as to whether or not force, or what is equivalent to force, was employed by the defendants. . . . Picketing may be lawful or unlawful. . . . The legitimate purpose of it [picketing] is to inform the strikers and their union as to what is going on at the plants. When it unnecessarily goes beyond this, and is conducted with the design and has the effect of intimidating those who may desire to remain at work or seek employment, it infringes upon human freedom and liberty of action. The right to work is protected by the law, as well as the right to quit work. . . . Whatever number of pickets was necessary to secure the reasonable and lawful purpose of the union is sanctioned by law, but where the number is swelled to 500 or 600, and at times to 1,000, . . . the unnecessary and unlawful purpose to awe and intimidate by numbers is apparent. Intimidation may consist in numbers alone without any actual violence. Many of the workers in plaintiff's factories were girls, and in such a case a large crowd of pickets, composed in part of women of foreign birth, with the calling of opprobrious names, and expressions and gesticulations of violence, would be sufficient alone to intimidate, without a single blow being struck.
>
> The picketing was not "peaceful." Names were called. Girls going to work had to pass through a line of pickets . . . , and "scab" and other opprobrious names, too vile to be mentioned, were called as they passed. No self-respecting woman would submit to such insults more than once.

On these facts, the judge awarded a permanent injunction and damages.[21]

Other cases displayed an even more pro-business orientation. In some cases, judges granted injunctions against strikes simply on the basis of allegations made in ex parte papers submitted by employers, without any hearing, trial, or findings of fact.[22] Others limited the purposes for which strikes could be called. One case, for example, held that workers could not strike for the purpose of compelling an employer to maintain a department of his business that he wished to close down,[23] and another enjoined a strike by a union that sought to require an employer to place a foreman, selected by the union, on every job, at great expense to the employer.[24] A final case occurring during World War I prohibited a strike against a shoe manufacturer, 80 percent of whose business was with the military.[25]

Thus, the law in regard to organizing, striking, and picketing was, like other bodies of New York law, mixed. Workers enjoyed important rights that enabled labor unions to exist and in some contexts to obtain substantial power. But the role of the courts in connection with specific strikes depended on the facts, and trial judges possessed significant discretion to find the facts however they wished, often contrary to the interests of workers and their unions.

Judicial Review of Pro-Labor Legislation

In addition to elaborating a common law based on principles of freedom of contract dealing with the rights to organize, strike, and picket, New York courts during the six decades after 1860 passed upon a great deal of legislation enacted in support of the labor movement. Again, the results were mixed.

The ambivalence of the court of appeals was clear in an early case, *Perkins v. Heert*,[26] which involved a challenge to the constitutionality of legislation creating a procedure for registration of union labels and making it unlawful to counterfeit those labels.

The challengers argued that the legislation was "unconstitutional and ... contrary to public policy, in that it unjustly discriminate[d] in favor of the labor of members of ... unions as against that of non-union workmen." They further asserted that the "act was procured for the purpose of enabling union labor organizations to boycott nonunion laborers and to deprive them of the legitimate fruits of their labors."[27]

The court of appeals found that the challenge was "serious and require[d] deliberate consideration."[28] The difficulty was that the argument of the challengers was true: the purpose of union labels was to drive nonunion employers out of business and force their employees to join unions. The principle of freedom of contract to which the court adhered—a principle that gave workers freedom to join or not to join unions and employers freedom to accept or to reject unionization of their businesses—thus required a decision in favor of the challengers, but the court's support for unions required the opposite. In the end, the court punted. It refused to "assume" that the purpose of the legislature was to aid union against nonunion workers or that unions would "resort to acts which are unlawful." It concluded that the act simply "allow[ed] the members of the union to send the products of their labors into the markets of the country marked in such a way as to indicate the character of their workmanship"—something "legitimate and proper."[29] On that basis, it upheld the legislation as constitutional.

With similar ambivalence, the court reached mixed results when it passed upon the constitutionality of legislation dealing with the rate of wages or the terms and conditions of their payment. It upheld, for example, a statute requiring railroads to pay employees semi-monthly and in cash.[30] And in *Clark v. State*,[31] it upheld a statute setting the rate of wages that the state or a subdivision thereof was required to pay its own workers in the context of a suit brought by a worker to recover that rate of pay. In *People ex rel. Rodgers v. Coler*,[32] however, it reached an arguably inconsistent result. There, a municipal contractor who had agreed in his contract with the city to pay the wage rate required by statute failed to pay it, but on completion of his work, he nonetheless brought suit against the city to recover the payment due him on the contract. The city's defense, which the court rejected, was the contractor's breach of contract.

The opinion of the court of appeals was profoundly unclear. On the one hand, the court found the statute inconsistent with the right of "the city and the contractor . . . to agree with their employees upon the measure of their compensation," and instead to "compel . . . them in all cases to pay an arbitrary and uniform rate."[33] The court in the *Clark* case limited the legislation's protection of workers; it ruled that the statute set only a default rate of pay that even a public employer and its employees were free to change at will, thereby effectively overruling the legislature's power to determine the pay rate. But later in the opinion, the court took a different approach. It spoke of the contractor's "claim to be paid what [was] justly due him" and suggested that the contractor had never "consented in the contract that it [the payment] should be forfeited to the city in the event of a violation of the Labor Law."[34] This reading suggested that the *Coler* case was only about the remedy for a failure to pay at the required rate. It suggested, that is, that an employee could sue his employer to collect his or her statutorily mandated pay, a just result, but that government could not act on the employee's behalf by refusing to pay for a contractor's completed work—also an arguably just result.[35]

In part, perhaps, because of *Coler*'s lack of clarity, the legislature proposed and the people of New York adopted an amendment to the state's constitution[36] authorizing legislative regulation of the wages and hours of workers employed on state and municipal projects. The court of appeals thereupon upheld New York City's refusal to pay a contractor whose employees had been required to work longer than eight hours per day in violation of a statute mandating such a limit.[37] The *Coler* case was thereby overruled. The court of appeals also upheld legislation requiring that all workers in the state be given a minimum of one day of rest in every seven.[38] A lower court held, however, that state legislation concerning maximum hours of railway workers was superseded by federal law,[39] and the court of appeals finally held that the legislation protecting workers on public projects did not apply on behalf of employees of subcontractors working outside New York, where wage rates were lower and working conditions different.[40]

A final subject of significant inconsistency was labor regulation on the basis of gender. In 1907 in *People v. Williams*,[41] the court of appeals struck down a statute prohibiting employment of women in factories before 6 a.m. or after 9 p.m. Although it recognized "that working in a factory in the night hours" was a "menace to the working woman,"[42] the court of appeals cited *Lochner v. New York*,[43] and declared that

> an adult female is not to be regarded as a ward of the state, or in any other light than the man is regarded, when the question relates to the business pursuit or calling. . . . She is entitled to enjoy, unmolested, her liberty of person, and her freedom to work, for whom she pleases, where she pleases and as long as she pleases, within the general limits operative on all persons alike . . . She is not to be made the special object of the exercise of the paternal power of the state. . . . In the gradual course of legislation upon the rights of a woman, in this state, she has come to possess all of the responsibilities of the man and she is entitled to be placed upon an equality of rights with the man.[44]

Six years later, in contrast, a state trial judge reached the opposite result in upholding a statute limiting the number of hours women and children could work.[45] He distinguished *People v. Williams* by relying on the Supreme Court's 1908 decision in *Muller v. Oregon*,[46] which, as he explained, "decided the fundamental proposition that, for the purpose of the application of a law under the police power, the Legislature may establish a class composed of women alone, and may limit the hours of labor of the individuals composing that class."[47] The judge then concluded:

> The pressure of women and children entering the industrial field in competition with men physically better qualified for the struggle[] has compelled them to submit to conditions and terms of service which it cannot be presumed they would freely choose. Their liberty to contract to sell their labor may be but another name for involuntary service created by existing industrial conditions. A law, which restrains the liberty to contract, may tend to emancipate them by enabling them to act as they choose, and not as competitive conditions compel. All these considerations are for the Legislature, and for the Legislature alone.[48]

The cases regulating women's labor laid bare the fundamental tensions and conflicts underlying all of turn-of-the-century labor law. On the one side was the right to work or to manage a business in one's own fashion and on one's own terms. As the son of a staunchly anti-union father whose ambition was to own his own business, I was taught to be independent and to lead rather than follow the crowd. I still value my freedom to pursue my own happiness and to strive to help others. As a historian, however, I have come to understand that many people cannot obtain the decency and dignity that are prerequisites to the pursuit of happiness except through collective effort. Similarly, turn-of-the-century judges understood the need of workers to act collectively through unions and through legislation.

Thus, New York judges recognized the right of workers to organize, strike, and picket but at the same time limited those rights so as to protect the liberty of employers and workers such as my father. Sometimes those judges upheld worker-protective legislation, but at other times they invalidated it. They understood that both workers and employers were entitled to the rights to liberty and to the pursuit of happiness while at the same time appreciating that society could create the foundation for those rights only through collective action.

Part Two

Facilitating Inevitable Legal Change

3

Business Law

Contract

The decades of the Civil War and after produced striking changes in the American economy. The law had to respond to those changes, and the New York courts did. On many occasions, however, the courts adhered to precedent, which at times favored business and the rich and at other times assisted the poor.

During the Civil War era, New York courts, according to Morton Horwitz, switched from a subjective, individual theory of contract to an objective theory.[1] In the early nineteenth century, contract theory had focused on the meeting of individual minds; people were held to contractual liability because they had actually agreed with another person to be so held. Early-nineteenth-century businessmen, for the most part, did deal with each other as individuals, and a jury could hear their testimony to determine what they had intended their contract to mean. Beginning in the 1860s, however, the economy began to change. Large national business corporations came into existence, especially in railroading. When representatives of two such corporations dealt with each other, it was no longer feasible to understand what the corporations actually meant when their representatives incorporated some term into a contract. The contract had to be interpreted, instead, on the basis of the standardized, objective meaning that the business community conferred on the terminology.

By placing his analysis of this switch to an objective theory of contract in a chapter that examines "the institution of contract" as "the legal expression of free market principles" that led to "enormously disproportionate market power" on the part of established elites[2]—a disproportion that progressives would later challenge[3]—Horwitz implied that New York judges behaved as pro-business conservatives. But, in fact, New York judges were in tune with the times and with established principles of American law. As far back as the colonial period, American judges had been tweaking the law so that it would not obstruct and at times would even facilitate economic development.[4] This policy was especially strong as courts strove to release economic energy in the first half of the nineteenth century.[5] And the policy continued into the second half of the century, with the court of appeals noting, for example, in the 1873 case of *Losee v. Buchanan*[6] that "factories, machinery, dams, canals and railroads" were "demanded by the manifold wants of mankind, and lay at the basis of all our civilization"[7] and in the 1881 case of *Barkley v. Wilcox*[8] that "restriction upon industry, and enterprise . . . should, we think, be determined largely upon considerations of public policy and general utility."[9]

Thus, the move of New York judges to an objective theory of contract in "increasingly utilitarian efforts to use law to promote economic growth"[10] was simultaneously conservative, in that judges continued to behave in the same fashion that judges had always behaved throughout American history, and forward-looking, in that as the structure of the economy changed, judges changed the law so as not to obstruct and at times even facilitate what economic growth required.

Another subject on which New York judges behaved both conservatively, in following practice that had taken root earlier in the century,[11] and progressively, in elaborating the law in accordance with emerging societal needs, was the law dealing with contracts in restraint of trade. Judges found monopolies and other contracts "in restraint of trade . . . illegal and void."[12] As Judge John Gray wrote for the New York Court of Appeals, "corporations are great engines . . . for the development of public wealth . . . , but if . . . permitted unrestrainedly to control and monopolize the avenues to that industry in which they are engaged, they become a public menace."[13] "Public policy," Gray continued, required "protection" against such menaces.[14]

Based on such concerns, New York courts declared contracts of the National Lead Trust, which had been "organized and carried on for the purpose of monopolizing the business of producing and selling various important products of lead . . . [,] contrary to public policy, and . . . 'void' and 'unlawful'";[15] contracts of the Onondaga Fine Salt Manufacturing Co., which had been organized "to limit and fix the amount of salt to be manufactured" and thereby "to fix and control the price thereof, . . . utterly void" and illegal;[16] contracts of the Milk Exchange, which was "a combination on the part of the milk dealers and creamery men in and about the city of New York to fix and control the price that they should pay for milk";[17] and a contract fixing prices between a comparatively small manufacturer of envelopes and the Standard Envelope Co., which manufactured 85 percent of the envelopes in the country, likewise void, even though the contract "so moderately advanced prices" that it "seem[ed] to some persons reasonable."[18] The courts also held a contract not to compete[19] and a contract to limit the quantity of coal shipped to a particular locality void as against public policy,[20] held criminal an effort of a cigarette company to monopolize the trade by intimidating wholesale dealers,[21] required telephone and telegraph companies to allow competitors unrestricted use of their lines,[22] and granted an injunction against newspaper publishers that had refused to provide newspapers to a dealer unless he agreed to carry in his stock all of the publishers' newspapers, some of which his customers did not wish to buy.[23]

Limits existed, however, to the opposition of New York judges to monopolies.[24] New York courts protected monopolies arising out of patents,[25] trade secrets,[26] and copyrights,[27] for example. They permitted a company to acquire one of its competitors "as a matter of prudence" to prevent "ruinous" competition that would lead to "the destruction of its business."[28] They also permitted railroads to merge,[29] to divide territories between themselves,[30] and to develop interchanges permitting continuous travel over multiple lines.[31] Finally, they upheld a rule of the New York Stock Exchange prohibiting members from transacting business on any rival exchange,[32] they allowed manufacturers to give rebates to retailers who sold their products at specified minimum prices,[33] and they permitted lumber companies to organize a secret arrangement to market their products.[34]

A most revealing case was *Park & Sons Co. v. National Wholesale Druggists Association*,[35] a 4–3 decision by the New York Court of Appeals. As the economy grew in the later decades of the nineteenth century, large companies that were able to outbid small competitors emerged. Ultimately the large companies were able to undersell the small ones and thereby drive them out of business. As this pattern emerged in the wholesale drug industry, with large wholesalers able to buy drugs from manufacturers at lower prices than small competitors could buy them, the small wholesalers organized the National Wholesale Druggists Association. The association then entered into contracts with manufacturers that required the manufacturers to sell to association members at the same price they sold to anyone else. In return, the association agreed that all retailers would sell drugs at prices set by the manufacturers.

Plainly these contracts authorized monopolistic price-fixing in restraint of trade. But a four-judge majority of the court of appeals nonetheless approved of the contracts. Although the majority "did not question the right of the big fish to eat up the little fish, the big storekeeper to undersell and drive out of business the little storekeeper," it "believe[d] that the little fellows have the right to protect their lives and their business, and if they can ... induce manufacturers to establish a uniform price for fixed quantities so that they can purchase as cheaply as the great merchants and thus compete with them in the retail trade, they have the right to do so."[36] The majority accordingly refused to declare the contracts contrary to public policy, void, and hence unenforceable.

The three-judge dissent also was concerned about "little fellows," not the small competitors for whom the majority had coined the phrase but other weaker individuals, namely, consumers. The dissenters focused on the provision in the contracts allowing manufacturers to set retail prices and noted how that provision eliminated competition and thereby raised the prices consumers would pay. Accordingly, the dissenters voted to hold the contracts void and unenforceable.

"Little fellows" also were protected in at least some cases in which the courts upheld covenants not to compete. A covenant not to compete was lawful and valid when it was "reasonable for the parties to enter into it" and "was a proper and useful contract, or such as could not be disregarded without injury to a fair contractor."[37] Thus, covenants were upheld when they enabled purchasers of a business or technology "to fully develop its business,"[38] when they protected a seller's "means of livelihood ... or means by which he gains the support of his family,"[39] or when they prevented abuse of a "confidential relationship."[40]

"Little fellows" finally were protected in a wide variety of other cases not involving issues of monopoly or restraint of trade. In other sorts of contract cases, the courts protected people who were "aged or infirm,"[41] people who were illiterate,[42] immigrants who knew no English,[43] and a woman who after separating from her husband had executed an agreement for support from her

father-in-law.[44] An entity whose agent had falsely assured the
other party that a written contract conformed to a preceding oral
agreement was not permitted to enforce the subsequent written
one and was thereby bound by the oral one.[45] The court of appeals
also upheld damage awards for consumers who were injured by
inherently dangerous products manufactured by defendants who
were not in privity with the consumers.[46]

New York courts also supported weaker parties to contracts by
invalidating many that were products of structurally unequal bargaining power. The leading case was *Johnston v. Fargo*,[47] in which
an employee of the American Express Company had agreed to a
provision exempting the company from liability for personal injuries suffered in the course of employment. The court of appeals
ruled the provision void, declaring:

> The employer and the employed, in theory, deal upon equal
> terms; but, practically, that is not always the case. The ar-
> tisan, or workman, may be driven by need; or he may be
> ignorant, or of improvident character. It is, therefore, for
> the interest of the community that there should be no en-
> couragement for any relaxation on the employer's part in
> his duty of reasonable care for the safety of his employees.
> That freedom of contract may be said to be affected . . . is
> met by the answer that the restriction is but a salutary one,
> which organized society exacts for the surer protection of
> its members.[48]

Lower courts adhered to these principles. One court, for instance,
held that the grossly unequal provision in major league baseball
contracts giving teams an option either to renew contracts from
year to year or to release players on ten days' notice made "the
baseball player . . . a chattel and therefore refused to enforce it."[49]
Another court held that when a creditor was compelled to accept
corporate stock worth less than what was owed in full payment of

a debt, a moral obligation survived to pay the remainder of what was owed and that the obligation constituted sufficient consideration to support a subsequent promise to so pay.[50]

Then there were contracts negotiated under temporary circumstances of inequality that took the form of duress. Thus, the court of appeals held that a promissory note or a promise not to sue obtained from a person in return for his release from an unlawful imprisonment was void for duress.[51] Later the court expanded its holding by ruling that any contract obtained under a threat of imprisonment, whether unlawful or lawful, of a spouse, parent, or child was void for duress.[52] Lower courts agreed.[53] Duress, however, often was difficult to prove. Thus, circumstances such as a threat to bring a suit initiated by a writ of capias,[54] a threat to file a mechanics lien,[55] an overwhelming need for a specific product,[56] or an overwhelming need to hire workers[57] were held not to amount to duress.

Other doctrines did not systematically favor "little fellows" but did limit how those who found themselves in positions of advantage could profit from that advantage. One such doctrine, which often aided people such as investors in corporate stock, was fraud.[58] Fraud, which consisted of any statement of a material fact known to be false by the person making it that induced the other party to enter into the contract, allowed that other party to avoid the contract.[59] Courts also held fraudulent a false statement made by a party without knowing whether or not it was true,[60] a statement on behalf of a third party made to an employer by an employee not known to be working for the third party,[61] and an agreement made by a creditor to gain advantage over other creditors who were unaware of the agreement.[62] But courts did not find fraud in cases in which a party acted under a mistake but no false statement had been made[63] or cases in which a managing partner purchased the interest of another partner.[64] They also held that a judgment creditor could not maintain an action for a fraudulent transfer of assets from a judgment debtor to a third person as long as the transfer occurred prior to the creditor's obtaining a lien on the assets.[65]

A second doctrine was illegality. Courts declared illegal contracts that sought to subvert or control the functions of officers or directors of corporations[66] or that sought to induce clients of a financial advisor to purchase stock being sold by a stockbroker with whom the advisor, unknown to the clients, had an agreement.[67] A major issue involved efforts, held to be illegal, to make money by getting government to adopt some policy or program, such as building a facility that would enhance the value of particular land[68] or procuring legislation that would affect the value of some stock.[69] It was permissible, however, to employ agents to obtain a government contract,[70] to draft and lobby for the passage of legislation,[71] or to settle a claim against the state.[72] Plea bargains in criminal cases also were upheld.[73] Of course, a contract to pay a woman $500 per month for support of a child born as a result of her agreement to have future intercourse with a defendant was illegal,[74] as was payment for housekeeping services provided by a woman who cohabited with a man, unless an express contract existed for such payment.[75]

A third doctrine was substantial performance. The leading case was Judge Benjamin Cardozo's 1921 opinion in *Jacob & Youngs, Inc. v. Kent*,[76] but that opinion was not without overwhelming precedent going back into the nineteenth century.[77] Sometimes, as in *Jacob & Youngs* itself, the doctrine of substantial performance assisted a "little fellow" contractor who was building a house for a wealthy individual, although that was not its explicit purpose.

In sum, the law of contract was mixed in its effects. The courts behaved conservatively in that they typically followed precedent while adapting contract doctrine to the needs of businessmen and to the ends of economic development. But their conservatism was not single-minded. Courts were also concerned with the well-being of "little fellows" and decided many cases to protect "little fellows'" interests.

The Legal Obligations of Corporations

As was noted above, New York judges understood that "corporations [were] great engines ... for the development of public wealth."[78] At the same time, however, the managers who controlled corporations possessed huge opportunities to cheat. For these reasons, New York corporation law between 1860 and 1920 carefully balanced the legal freedoms it granted to managers against the duties it imposed on them to prevent cheating of creditors, shareholders and investors, and third parties otherwise interacting with the corporations.

DUTY TOWARD CREDITORS

The basic rule—the rule of limited liability—that helped make corporations the economic engine that they were was that only the corporation and not its shareholders were responsible to creditors for the corporation's debts.[79] Shareholders, however, were individually liable for debts up to par value of their stock until the entire value of the capital stock was paid in.[80] "Little fellows" received special protection—shareholders were liable for wages due to laborers, servants, and apprentices.[81] And the assets of a corporation were viewed as a "trust fund for the payment of its debts"[82] so that if those funds were transferred out of the control of the corporation, creditors could collect their debts either from the men who authorized their transfer[83] or from the people to whom the assets were transferred.[84]

DUTY TOWARD SHAREHOLDERS AND INVESTORS: THE SEPARATION OF OWNERSHIP AND CONTROL

With the development of the corporate form of business organization, the old assumption that the owner of a business would manage and control it began to change. Ownership became separate from control, as "stockholders . . . [became] strangers to the management and control of the corporation business and affairs."[85] As a result, the corporation's officers and directors quickly gained the capacity to cheat or at least profit at the expense of the shareholder owners. New York courts responded with an attempt at balancing. They sought to limit cheating and profiteering while at the same time leaving managers in sufficient control of their corporate engines so as to enhance public wealth. Thus, in *Billings v. Shaw*,[86] the court of appeals reiterated the basic rule that officers and

> directors of corporations act in a fiduciary capacity. In every action where the interest of the corporation is involved, particularly where the same is in conflict with the individual interest of the [officers or] directors, they act as trustees and are strictly accountable to the . . . stockholders of the corporation for their action. . . . All acts of a director [or officer] in his own behalf when his personal interest is in conflict with that of the corporation are invalid at the election of the corporation.[87]

For this reason, a decision of a board of directors to dissolve a corporation had to be made in good faith in the belief that dissolution would benefit the company and its shareholders.[88] A director requesting extra compensation for his work as company secretary had to recuse himself when the board voted on his request,[89] as did a director seeking to sell property to the corporation.[90] The court of appeals also required officers who sold company property and secretly retained profits for themselves and some directors to disgorge those profits,[91] and the court ruled that a director who acquired for himself property that it was his duty to acquire for the corporation held the property in trust for the company.[92] Finally, the court held damage awards appropriate against directors of a corporation who lost or wasted corporate funds through negligence or inattention to their duties.[93]

Organizers of start-up firms were under a similar set of fiduciary duties toward their investors.[94] Investors "engage[d] in a common enterprise for their mutual benefit ... ha[d] the right to demand and expect from their associates good faith in all that relate[d] to their common interests.... No one of the subscribers [could] be permitted to take to himself a secret or separate advantage to the prejudice of his associates."[95]

Corporate managers and directors were forbidden to favor some shareholders over others.[96] For similar reasons, courts allowed minority shareholders to bring suit whenever a majority of the shareholders were engaged in an unlawful course of action that violated the minority's rights,[97] but only if it was "shown that the action of the governing body complained of [was] so clearly against the interests of the minority ... as to amount to a wanton and fraudulent destruction of the rights of such minority"—"that the action of the majority of the stockholders and directors [was] a clear, substantial, and flagrant violation."[98] Shareholders seeking to bring suit could not do so if they had ratified the action[99] or if the action had not been a wrong to the corporation.[100] Before suing directors for misconduct, shareholders had to request the corporation to sue unless the directors were in control of the corporation.[101]

The result of these cases was that officers and directors of corporations were, in large part, left free to run their businesses without interference by shareholders. They had power to employ people to run their businesses and to set their salaries.[102] They also had power to enter into contracts[103] even if the directors promoting a contract also served on the board of the other company with which the contract was made.[104] It was necessary only that managers act in good faith and in the interests of their company, not in their own personal interest, and whether they did so was a question of fact to be determined, if challenged, by a jury in a trial.[105]

DUTY TOWARD THIRD PARTIES: THE LAW OF PRINCIPAL AND AGENT

Corporations are incorporeal fictions and, as principals, can accomplish only the purposes for which they were created by employing human beings as agents. Third parties enter into transactions with those agents. Judges must then decide whether to treat those transactions as contracts or torts involving the third party and the corporation as principal, or as merely the third party and the agent as an independent individual functioning apart from any principal. Much of the basic law on this complex set of issues was elaborated in the period between 1860 and 1920.

In the small towns of early-nineteenth-century America, people knew nearly everyone in town and their relationships with one another. They could readily inquire whether another person with whom they were about to deal was acting on his or her own behalf or as an agent of some principal and, if so, what was the scope of the agent's powers. People could make individualized choices about whether to enter or to engage with people in agency relationships, and courts could determine liabilities on the basis of what factual inquiries into those possible relationships disclosed.

With the growth of population and the development of a national economy after the Civil War, however, inquiry into individualized business relationships became much too difficult. Businesspeople needed clear rules for planning how they should act, and courts needed clear rules for determining liability. Accordingly, the law turned from an individualized, will theory of agency, in which residents of small towns and members of small business communities focused on specific facts to determine the existence of an agency and the scope of an agent's powers, to an objective theory of agency, in which those matters were determined by examining whether a relationship fit within some standardized category.[106] The new approach became known as the doctrine of apparent authority. As the appellate division expressed the doctrine in a 1919 case: "Where an agent is intrusted to do a particular kind of business, he becomes, as between the principal and parties dealing with him, the general agent for the transaction of that business; and his acts, as between his principal and strangers, in that particular line, will bind the principal, although he violates some private instructions given by his principal not known to the public."[107] The doctrine went back, however, to the leading 1865 case of *New York & New Haven R.R. Co. v. Schuyler*,[108] in which the court of appeals had held that "sound and elevated morality" required that the principal be held liable. The question was not about which "one of two *innocent parties* . . . is to suffer." The moral principle was that when "somebody must be a loser by . . . [a] deceit, it is more reason that he that employ[ed] and put[] a trust and confidence in the deceiver, should be a loser than a stranger."[109]

Thus, when a mother authorized her son to buy and sell stock as an agent for her while she was in the United States and he continued to do so when she went to Europe, the court of appeals found him to have apparent authority as her agent and held that notices from brokers to him constituted notices to her.[110] Earlier, the court had held that an agent who had power to buy goods for his principal bound the principal to accept what he ordered even though a private instruction that he ignored required him to use printed blanks for the orders.[111] In another case, an insurance broker who had purchased policies for a sugar refinery in the past and was directed to buy another policy was held to be the agent of the refinery, which was bound by the policy he purchased.[112] A company that for a long time had sold products to another company whenever an employee of the latter company had ordered them was held to be justified in dealing with that employee as the latter company's agent.[113] A general manager of a stockbroker's branch office who received a check in payment for stock, forged an endorsement, and absconded with the money was held to be the broker's agent, and the payment for the stock was held to be good, even though the broker had never received it.[114] And, when a partnership engaging in the import business permitted a cousin of the partners to operate a flour business out of the firm's office, to use the firm name and letterheads, and to pay bills with the firm's checks, a third party dealing with the cousin was entitled to assume that he was an agent with apparent authority to bind the importing firm.[115]

On the other hand, a man who conducted a restaurant at a club was held not to be a general agent of the club and was held to have power to bind the club only in connection with the restaurant business.[116] A husband who delivered a deed to his wife's property as security for a loan to the husband was held not to be the wife's general agent with power to transfer title to her land.[117] And an agent who created a medical laboratory for an undisclosed principal was held to have authority only to create the laboratory and not to have power to donate it to a university of his choice.[118] Although courts were compelled to recognize the apparent authority of agents in order to enable corporations and third parties dealing with them to function efficiently and thereby facilitate economic growth, they reached the above results because they also remained committed to fundamental notions of fairness. Thus, the courts would apply the doctrine of apparent authority only when a principal did something to cause the appearance of authority[119] and only when a third person would suffer a loss if the courts did not apply it.[120] Courts also ruled that, if a person dealing with an agent had reason to suspect that the power of the agent was limited, the person was bound by the limitations.[121] Finally, any person making a claim about an agent's lack of authority was required to make the claim in a timely fashion.[122]

Another practice authorized by courts that facilitated the functioning of business permitted a person who, in fact, was acting as an agent to pretend he was acting for himself and to not disclose that he was acting for a principal. This practice enabled businesses to deal with third parties who would not deal with them or would deal only at a higher price than that at which they were prepared to deal with some agent. The legal rule was that a contract executed by an agent could be enforced by an undisclosed principal,[123] even if the contract would not have been made if the existence of the principal had been known.[124] The agent also could enforce the contract.[125] Again, however, along with their concern with business efficiency, New York courts cared about fairness. Thus, they would not allow an undisclosed principal to sue if his or her suit would cut off equities that existed between an agent and a third party.[126] And, since courts allowed either the undisclosed principal or the agent to enforce a contract, they also gave a third party a cause of action at his or her election against either the principal or the agent but not against both.[127] However, when a principal was known to a third party, the principal alone was liable on a contract, unless the contract specified that the agent also would be liable.[128]

Of course, if agents committed wrongful acts that caused damage to their principals, they were liable to the principals.[129] Likewise, if agents committed wrongful acts that caused damage to third parties, they as well as their principals were liable to those third parties.[130] Principals were liable even if they were totally innocent, on the basis of the equity rule "that where one of two innocent persons must suffer from the wrong or fraud of . . . [an agent], he must bear the loss whose action enabled the . . . [agent] to perpetuate the wrong or fraud."[131]

In connection with the law of corporations, as with the law of contracts, New York courts thus strove to balance economic development against fairness to ordinary people. With the understanding that corporations were powerful engines for generating public wealth, the law gave them limited liability, left their officers and directors free to manage their businesses largely as they wished, and allowed them as undisclosed principals to operate in secrecy. At the same time, the courts gave special protection to "little fellows" such as laborers and apprentices, otherwise required managers to act in good faith and in nondiscriminatory fashions, and made corporations liable for most acts of their agents. Ultimately, many matters, such as the good faith of managers and the authority of agents, became issues of fact at trial, and perhaps corporations, which may have had greater economic resources than many of their litigation opponents, enjoyed strategic advantages in the trial process. Unfortunately it is impossible within the scope of this study to know how prevalent those advantages may have been.

Thus, contract, corporation, and agency law witnessed a tension between doing what was needed to develop the state, its economy, and its well-being, on the one hand, and being fair to individual litigants, especially to the less well-off and less fortunate inhabitants of the state, on the other. New York's judges during the decades between the Civil War and World War I tried to do both, and, in their efforts, developed no clear balance between the two. In articulating contract, corporation, and agency law, the court of appeals gave business entrepreneurs the law they needed to develop the economy but at the same time required them to treat those with whom they dealt fairly and without fraud. The result was a body of doctrine that sometimes favored business entrepreneurs and the rich and at other times favored "little fellows"; the law was not consistent but lay somewhere in between.

4

Personal Injury Law

New York judges in the late nineteenth and early twentieth centuries were burdened in two respects that pointed them in a pro-business direction in deciding personal injury cases. The first respect was that people in the state suffered an enormous number of personal injuries, and courts, as a result, had to process a vast quantity of litigation. The second respect was that the judges inherited pro-defendant doctrine that in the absence of legislation or of abandonment of precedent pushed them toward conservative, pro-business decisions.

The Quantity of Injuries

America in the late nineteenth and early twentieth centuries was plagued by a huge number of personal injuries, especially in the workplace. John Witt has summarized the data. Around 1900, the annual rate of accidental death for the nation as a whole was one in every thousand people. In the workplace, one worker in every fifty was either killed or disabled for at least four weeks in a work-related accident. Some industries were especially dangerous. In 1890, for example, one in every three hundred railroad workers was killed in a workplace accident; among brakemen on freight trains, one in every one hundred was killed. Witt reports one estimate that 42 percent of railroad workers involved in the day-to-day operation of trains were injured annually on the job.[1]

Randolph Bergstrom has studied the impact of this huge number of injuries on litigation in one trial court—the Supreme Court of New York County. Personal injury cases increased from thirteen in 1870, to 112 in 1890, and to 595 in 1910—from 0.3 percent of all filings in 1870, to 2.4 percent in 1890, and to 9.7 percent in 1910. Comparable increases in personal injury litigation occurred elsewhere—in Boston from only about 12 suits in 1880 to about 1,400 in 1900 and in Cook County, Illinois, an 800 percent increase between 1875 and 1896. These statistics, however, underestimate the impact of personal injury litigation on judicial workload. When contested cases, which consume most of the time of judges, rather than mere filings are examined, the increase in New York County goes from five contested tort cases in 1870, to 21 in 1890, and to 70 in 1910—from 4.2 percent of all contested cases in 1870, to 18.4 percent in 1890, and to 40.9 percent in 1910.[2] Contested tort cases, nearly all of which involved personal injury, increased, that is, from less than one-twentieth of judges' workload to nearly one-half of that workload during the forty years between 1870 and 1910. Thus, it is not surprising that Elon R. Brown, an attorney in New York, complained in 1908 that "negligence cases [were] blocking . . . calendars with a mass of litigation so great as to impede administration in all other branches of law."[3] Concerns such a Brown's arguably led at least some judges to dismiss suits by injured plaintiffs as quickly as possible, without according plaintiffs the trials they needed in order to prove the damages they had suffered.

Inherited Precedent

In processing the personal injury half of their contested case load, New York's judges had to deal with a strong body of inherited, pro-defendant precedent. Three defenses that defendants could interpose—contributory negligence, assumption of risk, and the fellow-servant rule—are the most well-known doctrines that barred recovery of damages by injured plaintiffs.

It was black-letter law that a plaintiff could not recover damages for an injury resulting from negligence of a defendant if negligence of the plaintiff also contributed to the injury. The "rule [was] . . . too firmly settled in this state to be disturbed that the injury must have been occasioned solely by the negligence of the defendant, . . . that the person injured was free from fault which contributed to the accident, or the action is not maintained."[4] Thus, a "plaintiff who voluntarily exposed himself to a known danger could not recover for the [negligent] act" of a defendant or of a defendant's employee.[5] This was especially true for a plaintiff who exposed himself or herself to danger solely for the protection of property.[6] Moreover, the burden of proof on the issue of contributory negligence was on the plaintiff. "The absence of contributory negligence [was] part of the plaintiff's case, and the burden of satisfying the jury upon that point rest[ed] upon him."[7] Thus, if no evidence existed as to why a plaintiff had acted as he or she did, the plaintiff could not recover for a defendant's negligence.[8]

The second defense was assumption of risk. As the court of appeals declared in 1867, "when a man engages in a dangerous enterprise he accepts its ordinary risks and is bound to foresee and submit to the consequences which usually attend it."[9] Thus, a person who worked in a paper mill, who was familiar with the nature of pulp, and who was directed to shovel a mass of pulp about ten feet high onto a conveyer belt, assumed the risk that the mass of pulp would fall and injure him.[10]

The third defense was the fellow-servant rule. In a typical case, a motorman of a street railway car was injured in a collision with another car as a result of the decision of his conductor to take the car out on a wrong track on a foggy morning. On these facts, the court ruled that the accident was caused by the act of "the conductor in taking out the car on the wrong track on a densely foggy morning" and that the conductor's "negligence . . . [was] to be imputed to the plaintiff, whose fellow servant he was." Thus, the plaintiff was nonsuited.[11] The court of appeals reached a similar result in a case in which a man who was moving a four-and-a-half-ton safe was killed by the safe's falling on him as a result of the "negligence . . . [of] his co-servants and co-laborers, he participating with them in negligently doing the work they had in charge."[12]

Apart from these three defenses, other doctrines also stood in the path of injured plaintiffs' recovery of damages. One was proximate cause. When the evidence was undisputed about the several causes contributing to an accident, the question of which one was the proximate cause for which damages could be recovered was an issue of law for the court.[13] As a result of the legal nature of proximate cause issues, many judges felt free to dismiss complaints at the close of plaintiffs' cases.[14] Indeed, even after cases with disputed facts had been submitted to juries, which had then returned verdicts for plaintiffs, judges sometimes would intervene, set the verdicts aside, and grant new trials.[15]

What constituted a proximate cause? The court of appeals defined the concept in the leading case of *Laidlaw v. Sage*,[16] where it stated that "the proximate cause of an event must be understood to be that which, in a natural and continuous sequence, unbroken by any new cause, produces that event, and without which that event would not have occurred."[17] One trial judge was more pro-plaintiff, declaring in dictum that, when a new cause broke the chain of causation, a defendant who committed some initial "negligent" act could still be liable for a resulting injury when "according to common experience it [i.e., the negligent act] might, under the particular circumstances, have reasonably been expected to cause injury through the act of another."[18]

There were some cases in which it arguably could not be foreseen that some negligent act would be followed by a third-party act resulting in injury. Thus recoveries were denied in a case in which employees of the telephone company left on a public road a bottle of denatured alcohol that a nine-year-old boy picked up, lighted, and burned his younger brother with;[19] in a case in which employees of a defendant negligently failed to close a school door securely and a child who leaned against it fell into a cellar and died;[20] in a case in which a third party kicked a plaintiff sitting near a cellar that the defendant negligently had failed to close and thereby caused him to fall in;[21] in a case in which a stockyard negligently permitted a steer to escape and a third-party policeman who shot at the steer wounded the plaintiff instead;[22] and in a case in which a worker was in a location where it could not be foreseen that he would be struck by an iron beam that suddenly fell off a truck.[23]

There were other cases, however, in which the intervention of third parties was plainly foreseeable, and courts still excused negligent defendants.[24] In one case, for example, a defendant negligently left a loaded revolver in a bureau accessible to a third person, a thirteen-year-old boy, who took the gun and shot the plaintiff; only the third person who committed the criminal act was deemed responsible.[25] In another, a department store negligently left a swinging door at its exit, and when one shopper left the store, the door swung back, struck, and injured the plaintiff, but the department store nonetheless was held not liable.[26] And, in *Laidlaw v. Sage*,[27] the act of a third party was not only foreseeable but in fact foreseen. In that case, Russell Sage placed one of his employees between himself and a third party who was threatening him with a bomb, for the purpose and with the result that when the third party exploded the bomb, the employee rather than Sage was injured. The court of appeals nonetheless held that the bomber rather than Sage was the proximate cause of the injury even though Sage had moved the employee precisely because he foresaw that the bomber was about to attack him and because he wanted to use the body of the employee to protect himself.

Somewhat analogous to proximate cause was the issue of duty: a negligent defendant who injured a plaintiff would not be liable in damages if a court ruled as a matter of law that the defendant had no duty of care toward the plaintiff or had not breached its duty.[28] The key rule was that a property owner was under no duty of care toward trespassers, licensees, or other people on the property by the property owner's mere sufferance.[29] But defendants did owe a duty of care to any individual invited onto their property for their benefit, such as a business customer,[30] a passenger on a steamboat,[31] or an employee of a subcontractor who was injured while working to fulfill a contract entered into by a general contractor.[32]

A final obstacle in the path of a plaintiff's recovery of damages was the burden of proof. Absent proof of intentional or negligent infliction of injury, a plaintiff could not recover damages. As the court of appeals declared in an 1890 case against Standard Oil, the law did

> not impose the obligation of saving harmless others from the consequences resulting from the occurrence of inevitable accident. . . . As the existence of negligence is an affirmative fact to be established by him who alleges it as a foundation of his right of recovery, it was incumbent upon the plaintiffs to point out by evidence the defendant's fault, for the presumption is, until the contrary appears, that every man has performed his duty.[33]

A defendant could be held to liability "only on the ground of its negligence."[34] Thus, an owner of a building was not liable to a tenant killed by an elevator that started moving for some unaccountable reason,[35] and a farmer was not liable when a sudden gale of wind spread a fire to a neighbor's land.[36] Courts also held that it was not negligent to park a construction machine that was not dangerous on a public street,[37] to grossly understate the weight of a 19,000-pound object being shipped,[38] or to commit an act under the influence of a pressing danger that resulted in someone's injury.[39]

Taken together, the three inherited defenses of contributory negligence, assumption of risk, and the fellow-servant rule, the parallel doctrines of proximate cause and duty, and the standards as to burden of proof created a high hill to be climbed by victims of injury seeking to recover their damages. As a result, available statistics taken together for 1890 and 1910 indicate that plaintiffs won only slightly less than half of the personal injury suits they brought.[40]

Judicial Cracks in Inherited Doctrine

Although New York judges typically behaved conservatively by following precedents that denied recovery to victims of personal injury, they did not always do so. They appear to have understood that in particular cases justice required that injured people be assisted and compensated. Thus they sometimes modified rules, bent them, ignored them, and even overruled them in the interests of justice. Accordingly, the overall body of doctrine dealing with personal injury litigation was often inconsistent and was not nearly as conservative as inherited precedent dictated it ought to be.

Eckert v. Long Island R.R. Co.[41] was a most revealing case. Eckert died when he was struck by a train after successfully rescuing a three- or four-year-old child who had been on the railroad track as the train was approaching. The railroad claimed that the decedent was negligent in attempting the rescue, but the court decided in Eckert's favor. Justice simply demanded compensation for the family of a man who gave up his life to save the life of a child. It was the right thing to do, and the court, ignoring the law of contributory negligence, sustained a jury verdict compensating the decedent's family.

Minerley v. Union Ferry Co.[42] appears to be a case of minor contributory negligence that the court ignored, in this case because of the defendant's gross misconduct. In piloting his boat, the plaintiff had violated a statute requiring that all boats on certain portions of the East River be navigated as close as possible to the center of the river. The court ruled, however, that the plaintiff's violation of the statute "in no manner contributed to the happening of the accident"; it stated that the position he was in as a "consequence of his violation of the statute . . . gave no right to the other boats in the river to run him down."[43] The court, that is, seemed to reach the just result that apparently gross misconduct by the defendant overcame minor contributory negligence by the plaintiff.

Courts also ignored possible contributory negligence of plaintiffs in other cases in which the negligence of the defendant appeared to be far greater than that of the plaintiff.[44] They refused to hold young children guilty of contributory negligence[45] and would not allow the negligence of a husband to defeat his recovery in an action brought for the death of his wife.[46] Despite the rule noted above that motormen and conductors of street cars were fellow servants, courts often did not permit the negligence of one to interfere with recovery of damages by the other from their common employer.[47] As the court of appeals declared in one case involving issues of whether a motorman or a conductor was in control of a street car, it would "not take judicial notice of their relations for the purpose of reversing a judgment."[48]

New York judges also decided some proximate cause cases in a fashion inconsistent with the black-letter law discussed above. In

Lowery v. Manhattan Railway Co.,[49] fire fell from the defendant's locomotive onto a horse pulling a wagon on the street below and onto the driver of the wagon. The horse ran away, and the driver tried to stop the horse by driving onto the sidewalk, which caused the horse and wagon to run down the plaintiff. The railroad claimed that the driver's mismanagement of the horse was an intervening cause of the plaintiff's injury that rendered it free from liability. The court, however, ruled contrary to much preexisting law that "so long as the injury was chargeable to the original wrongful act of the defendant, it [was] not apparent . . . how it [could] avoid responsibility. There was no such intervening human agency as would authorize the conclusion that it was the cause of the accident."[50] Justice simply required that an innocent, injured plaintiff receive compensation from a grossly negligent defendant.

Sauter v. New York Central R.R. Co.[51] was another court of appeals decision. Mr. Sauter received a critical injury from which he would have died when a train jerked backward as he was exiting. He employed a competent and skillful surgeon to correct his injury, but he died when the surgeon was guilty of malpractice during the course of the surgery. The court concluded, however, that there was "no authority" for the "proposition" that it was "the surgeon and not the injury [that] killed him."[52] A trial court similarly held that when an employee was injured when he attempted to lift a barrel and slipped and fell against an unguarded fly-wheel belt, the cause of the injury was the lack of a guard on the belt, not the slip and fall. Justice required that result so that the employee who had suffered "very serious injuries" would be compensated.[53] Some cases even went so far as to hold that, if a defendant could have foreseen an injury resulting from its conduct, it was negligent and liable for a recovery in damages.[54]

More importantly, New York courts acted to lessen the burden of proof that injured plaintiffs had to sustain in order to win lawsuits. An important rule aiding plaintiffs during the nineteenth and into the early years of the twentieth century was the doctrine that violation of a statute or ordinance, although not negligence per se, was competent evidence of negligence sufficient to warrant submission of a case to a jury.[55] As the court of appeals explained in the 1879 case of *Willy v. Mulledy*,[56] "when a statute impose[d] a duty . . . , it [was] well settled that any person having a special interest in the performance thereof may sue for a breach thereof causing him damage." It was "a general rule, that . . . a breach of . . . duty causing damage gives a cause of action."[57]

As the years progressed, the courts' interpretation of the doctrine grew increasingly favorable toward plaintiffs. Twenty-four years after *Mulledy*, the court of appeals in *Marino v. Lehmaier*[58] reiterated the "general rule that whenever one owes another a duty . . . , any person having a special interest in the performance thereof may sue for a breach thereof."[59] Four years later, the appellate division went a step further, paraphrasing and citing *Marino* and adding a sentence declaring that a "violation of a duty imposed by a statute or ordinance" not only gave rise to a cause of action but constituted "evidence of negligence" sufficient to "justif[y] a jury in finding a verdict against a person who . . . violated the statute or ordinance."[60]

The year 1911 witnessed the key case of *Racine v. Morris*,[61] in which a police officer checking at night on an open building fell into an open elevator shaft and died. The issue was whether the owner of the building owed a duty of care toward the officer. The court assumed that no duty existed at common law, but it found that the New York City building code created a duty. It wrote that "the legislature may by statute create a duty unknown to the common law" and that the scope of that duty could "be answered only by the construction of" the statute. Given the "salutary and remedial" nature of the building code, the court thought it "incumbent upon us to give it a construction as broad and liberal as a reasonable and fair understanding of its language will permit."[62] Accordingly, it upheld a jury verdict for the officer's estate.

The court of appeals was still not ready, however, to hold that violation of a statute always constituted negligence. In the 1914 case of *Barr v. Green*,[63] a child was injured when she ran into a barbed wire fence that a defendant had constructed along the boundary of his property in violation of a statute requiring the written permission of adjacent landowners for the construction of such a fence. The court of appeals reversed a dismissal of an action to recover for the injuries but ruled only that the matter ought to go to a jury to determine whether, as a matter of fact, negligence had occurred.

Next came *Amberg v. Kinley*,[64] in which a factory worker died in a fire because the factory in which he worked did not possess a fire escape as required by the labor law. The trial judge charged the jury not that breach of the statute was evidence of negligence but that "the negligence of the defendant [was] established as a matter of law by his failure to provide a fire escape." "You have only to determine," the judge said, "whether or not the defendant's failure was the cause of the accident."[65] The court of appeals upheld the charge. It recognized that "whether a statute gives a cause of action to a person injured by its violation" or is merely "evidence, more or less cogent, of negligence which the jury may consider with all the facts proved depended on the purview of the legislature in the particular statute and the language which they have there employed." But it held in reliance on *Willy v. Mulledy* that "in a suit upon a cause of action . . . given by statute, it is not necessary for the plaintiff to prove negligence" and that "the failure to observe the statute create[d] a liability *per se*, or, as is otherwise and with less accuracy sometimes said, is conclusive evidence of negligence."[66]

Because the court of appeals had ruled that the effect of statutes depended on the intention of the legislature in connection with each one, some lower courts continued to hold that breaches of particular statutes were merely evidence of negligence, not negligence per se.[67] It was not until Judge Benjamin Cardozo's leading 1920 opinion in *Martin v. Herzog*[68] that the court of appeals made it plain that violation of a statute constituted negligence. There, the plaintiff had failed to place lights on the rear of the buggy in which he was riding at night and, as a result, was struck from behind by an automobile whose driver failed to see him. Cardozo wrote:

> We think the unexcused omission of the statutory signals is more than some evidence of negligence. It *is* negligence in itself. . . . To omit, willfully or heedlessly, the safeguards prescribed by law for the benefit of another that he may be preserved in life or limb, is to fall short of the standard of diligence to which those who live in organized society are under a duty to conform. That, we think, is now the established rule in this state. . . . In the case at hand, we have an instance of the admitted violation of a statute intended for the protection of travelers on the highway. . . . Yet the jurors were instructed in effect that they were at liberty in their discretion to treat the omission of lights either as innocent or as culpable. . . . Jurors have no dispensing power by which they may relax the duty that one traveler on the highway owes under the statute to another. It is error to tell them that they have. The omission of these lights was a wrong. . . . No license should have been conceded to the triers of the facts to find it anything else.[69]

By so holding that violation of a statute prescribing a safety measure constituted negligence per se, the court of appeals simplified plaintiffs' cases. Once a plaintiff could show that violation of a statute produced an injury and that the defendant had no available defenses, there was no point to a trial on the merits. The parties could simply bargain about the measure of damages. Settlement thereby became easier, and court calendars became less congested. The fact that potential defendants knew that they would face damage liability if they did not comply with safety legislation also helped to produce compliance with the legislation. *Martin v. Herzog* was accordingly a profoundly progressive decision.

The doctrine of res ipsa loquitur was likewise progressive in that it obviated the need of plaintiffs to prove negligence. As the court of appeals declared in 1874, "Where the thing is shown to be under the management of the defendant or his servants, and the accident is such as, in the ordinary course of things, does not happen if those who have the management use proper care, it affords reasonable evidence, in the absence of explanation by the defendant, that the accident arose from want of care."[70] On this basis, the court ruled that when a building, in the absence of explanatory circumstances such as a sudden wind storm, collapsed into the street, its owner was guilty of negligence and liable to pay damages to those who were injured. In subsequent cases, New York courts similarly applied res ipsa loquitur to award damages to a passenger on a train who was resting his arm on the sill of an open window when he was struck by a swinging door on a passing freight train,[71] to the estate of a rider in an elevator that descended so rapidly that it crashed and caused counterweights to fall through the roof of the elevator and kill the rider,[72] and to a person on a city sidewalk who was struck by a sign that unexplainedly and suddenly fell from an adjacent building.[73] Another rule, derived in this instance from the common law, allowed laborers to recover damages when their employers provided them with defective appliances.[74] A final rule assisting plaintiffs allowed suit and recovery of full damages against a negligent defendant even if a third party was also guilty of negligence; a plaintiff, that is, was given a choice in cases involving joint tortfeasors of suing one or however many of them the plaintiff wanted.[75]

In short, the law applied by New York courts in personal injury cases was not uniformly pro-defendant. Courts often decided cases in favor of plaintiffs. New York judges throughout the 1860–1920 period accordingly arrived at a mixture of conservative and progressive results, although that may not have been what they were seeking to accomplish. They may have been more concerned with such goals as obeying the law by following precedent and effectuating legislative policies, as doing justice in individual cases, and as attaining efficiency in the processing of their case load. Whatever the goals of New York's judges, however, the jurisprudence they bequeathed in personal injury law mixed progressivism in pursuit of justice with a conservativism that sometimes merely followed precedent but at other times also furthered the interests of business entities.

Public Opinion, the Jury, and Legislation

While the judiciary with relative constancy proclaimed a mixed jurisprudence producing both conservative and progressive results, public opinion between 1860 and 1920 grew increasingly progressive. As the rate of accidents continued to increase during the course of the six decades, different people took different steps to compensate the injured and to slow the rate of accident growth. And, as more and more people took various steps, public opinion increased in support of preventing accidents that could be avoided and compensating the victims of those that were unavoidable.

People who suffered personal injuries in the workplace were the least successful of all personal injury litigants in winning compensation. Forty-eight percent of all personal injury plaintiffs in the Supreme Court of New York County in the combined years 1870, 1890, and 1910 won their cases. But only thirty-one percent of those who suffered workplace injuries were successful, compared with fifty-four percent of those who were injured other than in the workplace. Indeed, in the earliest years after the Civil War, workers understood that their chance of winning lawsuits was so low that few even bothered to sue.[76] Informal help from employers and fellow employees is what most injured workers were left to rely on.[77]

Change began to occur, however, in the years around 1870, when the Ancient Order of United Workmen, which had been founded in 1868, began to provide insurance for members killed or disabled in workplace accidents. In the next few years, the United Workmen developed mainly into an organization for insuring its working-class members. Other cooperative insurance associations soon emerged, with the result, as John Witt has observed, that a "vast cooperative disability and life insurance movement . . . sprang up practically overnight in post-Civil War America." According to Witt, the "cooperatives" had become "more important" by the 1890s "in terms of number of policies and total insurance in force than the commercial life insurance industry, stock and mutual companies combined" and "the leading source of systematic compensation for accidental disability and death," with nearly one in every three workingmen in a state like New York covered by cooperative insurance.[78] As a result, New York's working class came to understand that, if a worker was injured on the job, he or she ought to receive and, in many cases, could expect to receive compensation for the damages resulting from the injury.

Beginning in the 1880s, another approach to workplace accidents also started to develop. A new generation of managers sought to promote workplace efficiency by reducing accidents and compensating and thereby rehabilitating workers who were injured. As one Wisconsin conservationist who understood it was efficient to use as few resources as possible in producing goods observed, "man himself should be conserved." This writer found "losses of life by accidents . . . appalling" and argued that "by proper precautionary measures . . . accidents may be reduced."[79] Managers who agreed accordingly sought to promote safety practices in their industries and to compensate injured workers,

at least in part because the provision of compensation would en-
courage the adoption of safety practices that were less expensive
than the payment of compensation.

Railroads were first to establish compensation funds. The Baltimore and Ohio Railroad established such a fund in 1880, the
Pennsylvania Railroad in 1886, the Reading Railroad in 1888, and
the Chicago, Burlington, and Quincy Railroad in 1889. By the
end of the 1890s, more than one in every five railroad workers was
covered by an accident relief fund. Other industries followed suit:
United Traction and Electric in 1901, General Electric in 1902,
Westinghouse in 1903, New York Edison in 1905, and Swift and
Company in 1907.[80] These companies found it necessary to do so
because failure to compensate for injuries produced "discontent,
class feeling, and an impression of injustice."[81] By the beginning
of the twentieth century, in short, employers had come to understand along with employees that, if a worker was injured on the
job, he or she ought to receive and, in many cases, could expect to
receive compensation for the damages resulting from the injury.

The growing understanding that injured workers, along with
other injured people, should and often would receive compensation also affected the manner in which juries decided cases. Randolph Bergstrom, who studied jury verdicts in three years—1870,
1890, and 1910—found a clear shift in how jurors approached
cases. At the beginning of his period of study, people thought individuals to be responsible for their own fate. When they injured
themselves on broken sidewalks or loose floorboards or in dark
hallways, for instance, they tended not to sue, accepting responsibility for their own injuries. Contributory negligence mattered.
In later years, in contrast, jurors consistently placed responsibility
on people who created such conditions as broken sidewalks, loose
floorboards, and dark hallways or otherwise indirectly caused injury.[82] Defendants came to be expected to foresee the remote
consequences of their actions. This shift in popular conceptions
that was reflected in jury behavior caused conservatives with val-

ues still rooted in the past to criticize juries for "general prejudice against . . . companies"[83] and for being "even anarchistic in their ideas . . . especially against capital and vested interests."[84]

The growing understanding that people, often of limited means, who suffered injury at the hands of prosperous businesses should be compensated by those businesses had an impact finally on politics and legislation. As is shown by the cases discussed above that address the issue of whether violation of safety legislation constituted negligence per se or merely evidence of negligence,[85] the legislature enacted a significant amount of safety legislation between 1860 and 1920. An especially important piece of legislation was the Employer's Liability Act of 1902,[86] which abolished the fellow-servant rule in regard to coworkers who acted as supervisors. Prior to the act, the fellow-servant rule barred recovery of damages by a worker who was injured when obeying a negligent order of a supervisor. The 1902 act, in contrast, treated the supervisor as an employer, not as a fellow servant.[87] The act also modified the doctrine of assumption of risk by making employers liable for a dangerous condition created by their negligence unless the condition was known only to workers and the workers failed to report it to their supervisors.[88] Four years later, the legislature passed the Barnes Act,[89] which made railroads responsible for most railroad injuries. This 1906 act overturned the fellow-servant rule in connection with all workers who controlled trains, switches, and signals and made the railroads responsible for any negligence committed by those workers. The act also applied the doctrine of res ipsa loquitur to all cases in which an injured railroad employee proved the existence of any defect in a train, switch, or any other machinery or material provided by the railroad.[90]

The ultimate achievement of the legislature, of course, was the enactment of a workers' compensation law in 1910,[91] which abolished the common law defenses of contributory negligence, assumption of risk, and the fellow-servant rule and required compensation for all workplace injuries regardless of causation or fault.[92] In the next year, however, the court of appeals in *Ives v. South Buffalo Ry. Co.*[93] declared the 1910 legislation unconstitutional. But two years later, the people of the state of New York, reflecting the "feeling which pervaded the community generally, including both jurors and judges, that business should bear the loss of the injury to human as well as inanimate material ... , without too curious an inquiry into the cause,"[94] overwhelmingly approved an amendment to the state constitution authorizing the enactment of workers' compensation legislation,[95] and the legislature promptly enacted a new law.[96] In 1915, the court of appeals upheld the constitutionality of the new law in *Jensen v. Southern Pacific Co.*[97] and the Supreme Court of the United States agreed, although it refused to apply the statute to the particular worker injured in that case.[98]

In conclusion, it appears that various entities participating between 1860 and 1920 in the development of New York's personal injury law made both conservative and progressive contributions to that law. Judges, concerned with following precedent, doing justice in individual cases, disposing of their caseloads efficiently, and giving effect to legislative policies, made both conservative and progressive additions to the law. Jurors, concerned with doing justice to their peers—ordinary people like themselves—probably had a mainly progressive input. And the legislature, bound to follow increasingly progressive public opinion, periodically made progressive changes in the law and ultimately transformed an entire, major segment of it—the segment dealing with injuries in the workplace. New York's personal injury law thus was never the overwhelmingly conservative body of doctrine that historians have often thought it to be.

Part Three

Adherence to Precedent and the Past

5

The Law of Pleading and Civil Procedure

One Form of Action

In 1848–1849, the New York legislature took a radically progressive step by adopting a code of civil procedure, of which David Dudley Field was the principal draftsman. The Field Code abolished common law pleading with its writs and forms of action. It also put an end to jurisdictional and procedural divisions between the common law and equity. In place of these centuries-old divisions and distinctions, the legislature declared that "hereafter" there would be only "one form of action" called a "civil action." To commence an action, a plaintiff needed only to state "the facts constituting the cause of action, in ordinary and concise language, without repetition, and in such a manner as to enable a person of common understanding to know what is intended."[1]

New York judges, however, interpreted the new code conservatively. Indeed, some judges treated the new code with disdain. Justice Seward Barculo, for one, "regretted, that those who assumed the responsibility of devising a remedy for the insufficiencies of the former system, did not more fully understand and appreciate the true cause and nature of the evils to be remedied." As a result, "alteration [was] mistaken for reformation," with a failure to distinguish "between the benefits of a solid reform, and the crude innovations of conceited pretension."[2] When it was argued in a later case that his "construction" of a provision "repeal[ed] the Code," he responded that, if that "were true," he would "deem it not an unpardonable offence." In his view, the code "repeal[ed] itself" by "meddling with a subject not understood" and coming "into collision with 'a higher law,'—the law of nature—which it cannot overcome."[3] Justice Henry Welles, in turn, "deplore[d] the spirit of innovation, which, for the last two sessions ... govern[ed] the counsels of our Legislature on the subject of legal practice and pleading."[4]

Criticism by other judges was somewhat gentler. Justice John Edmonds spoke of "the many questions of doubt and difficulty ... which flow[ed] from the imperfect and inartificial use of the language in which" the code was "expressed."[5] Justice Samuel Lee Selden worried that "the science of legal pleading [was] broken up,"[6] with the result, in the words of Justice Augustus C. Hand, that without "settled principles by which good pleading is tested, ... doubt, uncertainty, and perplexity, to say nothing of constant novelty and diversity, [would] tend to render the administration of justice at least tardy, precarious and irregular, if not capricious."[7]

Three problems, in particular, plagued the judiciary. The first was the issue of how specifically and in how much detail the facts constituting the cause of action needed to be pleaded. Could a plaintiff plead, for example, merely that a defendant committed fraud? Or did the plaintiff need to recite all the details of his transaction with the defendant? Or something in between? The new code did not say. Judges therefore turned to what they understood to be the traditional science of pleading. Justice Hand, for example, wrote that the code "abolished all the *forms* of pleading theretofore existing, but did not abolish the fundamental principles" of pleading, as set out in treatises that he cited.[8] Pleading both the plaintiff's cause of action and the defendant's ground of defense consisted, according to Hand, of a statement of facts "in an intelligible and issuable form, capable of trial . . . , not the mere evidence of those facts . . . , nor matter of law only." He urged lawyers to "use . . . simple and settled forms of issues . . . to which juries can generally respond, yea or nay."[9]

Justice Edmonds agreed that "the principles of pleading [were] left untouched by the code." Under those principles, "the pleader did not set out . . . all his probative facts . . . , but only the legal conclusion which was properly deducible from them." Without those principles, Edmonds continued, "it would often be difficult to form any issue as soon as the reply, and when formed it would often be on some quite immaterial point."[10] Justice Selden similarly could not "persuade" himself "that the legislature could have intended to abrogate principles of pleading designed to develop and present the precise point in dispute, upon the record itself, without requiring any action on the part of the court." The purpose of pleading, he explained, was to generate "a single *material* issue, either of law or of fact, the decision of which would dispose of the case."[11]

These judges all urged lawyers not to "depart[ ] from the old and well established form[s] of a count" that they had used in common law pleading. Justice Edmonds gave an example. Assume that a plaintiff lent his horse to a defendant who refused to return it on demand. If the plaintiff merely wanted his horse back, he should plead the words he would have used in a common law action of replevin. If he wanted damages, including consequential damages, he should plead the words he would have used in trover. If he wanted the value of the horse, he should plead the words of assumpsit, that he sold and delivered the horse.[12] This conservative determination that the principles of pleading were not changed by the Field Code remained good law throughout the nineteenth and into the twentieth century, as the cases just discussed continued to be cited.[13] Indeed, as one later nineteenth-century case declared, "the facts required by the Code to be stated in pleadings are such facts as were required to be stated in pleadings at the common law."[14]

More difficulty arose from the second problem that troubled the judiciary—the merger of common law and equity. Before the enactment of the Field Code, common law pleadings had been brief and formalistic, whereas equity pleadings had set out facts in great detail. The code, however, created only one form of action and one set of rules of pleading for all cases. According to the 1851 case of *Williams v. Hayes*,[15] "it was not the intention of the legislature, in adopting the Code, to continue the distinction between common law and equity pleadings. On the contrary, it was intended that there should be but one system of pleadings."[16] *Millikin v. Cary*,[17] decided the previous year, explained the reason. It noted that before the adoption of the code, lawyers had to decide whether to bring a suit at common law or in equity and that, if they made the wrong judgment, their suit would be dismissed. If they had to choose under the code whether to file a pleading in a common law or an equity format, they would face the same dilemma. Accordingly, *Millikin* and *Williams* held that the legislature had adopted a single form of pleading for all cases.

In *Rochester City Bank v. Suydam*,[18] Justice Samuel Lee Selden disagreed. He explained "that the section of the Code which require[d] every complaint to state the *facts* constituting the cause of action" did not determine whether a complaint for equitable relief needed to be "drawn in the condensed form required by the rules of the common law, or with all the elaborate detail which the practice of the Courts of Chancery warranted." The way to determine the answer, in his view, was "to look into the reasons which led" historically "to the adoption of different modes of stating facts in the courts of equity and common law."[19] "Trial by jury" was the reason why "the common law system of pleading was constructed" as it was; issues had "to be presented to a jury" in a "single" manner that would be "decisive of the right."[20] But the kind of relief afforded by a court of equity, imperatively required a different mode of stating the case from that adopted in the common law courts.

The decree in chancery with all its varied provisions, its conditions, and limitations could not be engrafted upon the record of a common law action. The two were incompatible. From the one, was carefully excluded every fact not essential to enable the court to determine *for which party* to give judgment. The other required a consideration of all the circumstances bearing upon the nature of the judgment, and going to *modify* or *vary* its provisions.[21]

Selden accordingly concluded that as long as the courts were "permitted to adapt the relief they afford, to the facts and circumstances in one class of cases, while they are confined to a simple judgment for or against the plaintiff in all others, . . . different rules [must] be applied to pleadings at law and in equity."[22] Selden reiterated this position in a later case,[23] and other judges agreed with him.[24] Complaints for equitable relief accordingly continued to contain detailed presentations of facts for the rest of the nineteenth century and into the twentieth.[25] And, for essentially the same reason that actions at law were tried by a jury and actions in equity were tried by the court, judges ruled conservatively that actions at law and actions in equity could not be joined in the same suit.[26] As the court of appeals declared in 1881, "the distinction between legal and equitable actions is . . . fundamental, . . . and no legislative fiat can wipe it out."[27]

The courts, in fact, had no choice but to behave conservatively. The Field Code had abolished the old forms of action and created a single new action, but a third problem that plagued judges was that the code did not replace the substantive law that had been implicit in the interstices of the old forms. Thus the courts had to turn to old substantive law to know what facts plaintiffs needed to plead and prove to win their cases and what remedies were available. As Samuel Lee Selden, now a judge on the court of appeals, wrote in the 1860 case of *Goulet v. Asseler*,[28] the code had "abolished all distinction between the mere forms of action." But the "actions var[ied] in their nature, and there [were] intrinsic differences between them." He continued that "substantial differences remain[ed] as before. The same proof, therefore, [was] required in each of" the various actions "as before the Code, and the same rule of damages appl[ied]."[29] In the years to come, courts accordingly continued to have to refer to the old common law categories such as "trover" and "replevin."[30] With the judiciary's conservative applications of David Dudley Field's radical code, the forms of action were gone, but the common law derived from the forms remained in place.

Counterclaims

The Field Code also made changes in the rules relating to counterclaims. Before enactment of the code, the doctrines of setoff and recoupment allowed a defendant to reduce the amount of a plaintiff's judgment up to any amount owed by the plaintiff to the defendant. But a defendant could not recover any judgment against a plaintiff for any excess above the amount for which the plaintiff was suing. For example, if plaintiff and defendant were merchants who traded with each other and the plaintiff sued the defendant for $1,000, then the defendant could reduce the plaintiff's judgment to $200 if the plaintiff owed the defendant $800. If the plaintiff owed $1200, the defendant could reduce the plaintiff's judgment to $0, but he or she could not obtain a judgment against the plaintiff for the $200 the plaintiff still owed. To recover that $200, the defendant would have to bring a separate suit.

The Field Code allowed a defendant to file a counterclaim and obtain a judgment for an amount in excess of the plaintiff's claim in either of two circumstances: (1) if the defendant's claim arose out of the same transaction that gave rise to the plaintiff's claim[31] or (2) if the plaintiff brought suit on a contract and the defendant's claim was based on a different contract existing at the time the plaintiff brought suit.[32] Unlike the manner in which they dealt with the legislature's creation of a single form of action, New York's judges interpreted the new counterclaim rules generously.

As the Appellate Division declared, "the practice prescribed by the Code is intended to secure adjustment in a single action of all controversies between parties concerning the same subject matter, and to that end a liberal construction of its provisions in relation to the counterclaims, which may be interposed, may be indulged."[33] The court of appeals agreed in analyzing the doctrines of setoff and recoupment. Such doctrines, in its view, "promote[d] justice and diminish[ed] circuity of litigation. Courts and legislatures deem[ed] them remedial in character and the rules creating and regulating them entitled to a construction fairly liberal."[34]

Thus, when a subcontractor sued a general contractor for payment for work done, the general contractor was permitted to deduct from the amount due sums adjudicated against him that he had paid as compensation to third parties for the subcontractor's negligent work.[35] When an occupant of property sued a defendant for wrongfully cutting down trees and taking a quantity of wood, the defendant was allowed to counterclaim that it held a mortgage on the property and that the plaintiff was intending to reduce or deprive the defendant of the value of its security.[36] When another plaintiff sued to recover a balance due for work done, the defendant was allowed to counterclaim to recover the cost of having the work completed by another contractor.[37] And when a plaintiff sued to prevent interference with his use of a wharf, the defendant was allowed to counterclaim that he owned the wharf and that the plaintiff was a trespasser.[38] In all these cases, it could "with great propriety be said that [the] defendant's claim had some connection with the subject of the [plaintiff's] action." That connection could be "slight or intimate, remote or near," but as long as it was "just and equitable that the controversy between the parties as to the matters alleged in the complaint and in the counterclaim should be settled in one action by one litigation,"[39] New York courts would lean toward permitting the filing of the counterclaim.

Courts also were liberal in regard to pleading rules respecting counterclaims. The court of appeals held, for example, that a counterclaim did not need to contain all the facts needed to constitute its cause of action; those facts could appear elsewhere in the defendant's answer or even in the plaintiff's complaint.[40] Generally, courts allowed a defendant to bring his or her claim either as a counterclaim or in a separate action,[41] although separate suits were occasionally barred when a litigant failed to present a defense or file a counterclaim in an initial action.[42] Of course, a counterclaim could not be filed if the plaintiff was not obligated on the counterclaim.[43] Once a counterclaim was filed, the original plaintiff could defend against it but could not file a counterclaim to the counterclaim.[44]

Service of Process and Imprisonment for Debt

At common law, a plaintiff's right to imprison a defendant for debt was connected to the mode chosen by the plaintiff to serve process. If a plaintiff served process by a writ of capias, under which a defendant was arrested and required to give bail, the plaintiff without further judicial intervention could execute a judgment against the defendant, if the judgment could not otherwise be satisfied, by having the defendant imprisoned for debt. If, however, the plaintiff served process by summons or by attachment of a defendant's property, imprisonment for debt was not available without a further judicial order.

When the New York legislature in 1831 abolished imprisonment for debt, it prohibited service of process by arrest in simple breach of contract cases, although arrest remained available in tort actions.[45] What happened if a plaintiff joined two claims in a single action—assumpsit, a form of action for breach of contract, and case for negligence, a form of action in tort for damaging the subject matter of the contract? *Brown v. Treat & Carter*[46] adopted a pro-debtor rule that because the plaintiff had sued in contract, he could not serve process by arrest even though he also had joined a claim in tort. This rule interpreted the 1831 statute in an expansive pro-debtor fashion. The same case also declared in an even more pro-debtor dictum that, when a plaintiff had a choice of suing either in assumpsit or in trover, he was not free to sue in tort and thereby arrest the defendant; if a case could be brought in contract, it had to be so brought for purposes of service of process. *Suydam v. Smith*,[47] however, disagreed with this dictum and held in a less expansive, more pro-creditor fashion that, if trover would lie without the joinder of a claim in assumpsit, a plaintiff could elect to sue in tort alone rather than in contract. The plaintiff could thereby serve process by arrest even though the underlying suit was fundamentally for breach of contract.

Following enactment of the Field Code, the court of appeals in an 1849 dictum upheld the pro-debtor rule adopted by the 1841 court in *Brown v. Treat & Carter*.[48] But three years later in *Corwin v. Freeland*,[49] the court effectively overruled itself and interpreted the code in a pro-creditor fashion by holding that, even if a plaintiff pleaded only a breach of contract in his complaint, he could request a judge to issue an order for the defendant's arrest by filing an affidavit alleging that the defendant had obtained the goods involved in the suit by fraud, a tort. The *Corwin* case thus overturned the early expansive, pro-debtor interpretation of the 1831 legislation abolishing imprisonment for debt by ruling, in effect, that a creditor could join a tort affidavit to a contract pleading and thereby proceed in a contract case toward ultimate imprisonment for debt. This case law was, in general, followed throughout the nineteenth century.[50]

It is difficult to determine how conservative or progressive this case law was. In the ordinary debt case in which a debtor was not guilty of any fault, such as fraud or negligence, the debtor could not be arrested or imprisoned. In such cases, the courts interpreted the 1831 act and the 1848 code progressively and consistently with the legislature's intent. But what about cases in which the debtor committed fraud or damaged goods and then refused to pay for them? Was it conservative or progressive to allow such debtors to be imprisoned? Or were judges simply weighing the comparative fault of wrongdoers? Who was worse: Scrooge-like creditors or perpetrators of fraud? The case law does not tell us what was in the minds of judges.

The Fact-Finding Power of Juries

New York judges decided many cases upholding the power and right of juries to decide questions of fact. The case law was clear that when the evidence presented an issue of fact, a court could not nonsuit a plaintiff or direct a verdict but was required to submit the case to the jury.[51] When "the conclusion to be reached depended upon the credit which should be given to the several witnesses and the inferences to be drawn from their testimony," it was "a conclusion which the court should . . . allow[] the jury to draw."[52] "It [was] not enough to justify a nonsuit" or a directed verdict that a court "might grant a new trial. It [was] only where there [was] no evidence in law . . . [to] sustain a verdict" that a court could nonsuit a plaintiff or direct a verdict.[53] Only where no conflict existed in the evidence as to material facts or in the inferences to be deduced from the proven facts was it proper for a court to direct a verdict.[54] When it "[could] not be conceived that reasonable men would differ . . . [,] the court, as an administrative necessity," could remove a case from a jury and thereby promote the efficient processing of cases.[55] A court could also direct a verdict if both parties requested it to do so.[56]

If judges were dissatisfied with a jury's verdict in a case in which there was evidence on both sides, the property remedy was to grant a new trial before a new jury. But even in this regard, the freedom of judges was limited. As one 1865 case declared:

When there is a conflict of evidence, the court will not grant a new trial on the ground that the verdict is against evidence, even though they deem the conclusion reached by the jury erroneous. . . . To set aside a verdict . . . there must be such a preponderance of evidence as to satisfy the court that there was either an absolute mistake on the part of the jury or that they acted under the influence of prejudice, passion or corruption.[57]

A concurring judge agreed that, although his "impression [was] strong that the verdict was not in accordance with the real truth of the case," he did not find "the case . . . so flagrant as to show passion, prejudice or inattention to their duty, on the part of the jury,"[58] and therefore he too was unwilling to set the verdict aside. The standard of proof required to show passion or prejudice was quite high, as demonstrated by cases in which a Chinese plaintiff and a Jewish plaintiff claimed prejudice and their claims were denied.[59] Another court found nothing improper in two jury verdicts for a plaintiff who was prosecuted for but acquitted of committing perjury during his two trials and whose chief witness confessed to lying; that court nonetheless refused to set the two verdicts aside.[60]

The court of appeals was equally clear that in "a case where the facts, or inferences to be drawn from them, were in some degree doubtful, . . . the only proper rule under such circumstances [was] to submit the whole matter to the jury with proper instructions."[61] Lower courts also agreed. One case, for example, noted that "where there [was] evidence in support of" a verdict, "it [was] not, as a rule, the province of the court to set [it] aside,"[62] and another case declared that the "mere fact that the trial justice thought the jury drew the wrong inference did not warrant him in setting aside the verdict as against the weight of evidence" when "the inference adopted by the jury was fairly warranted by the evidence."[63] Other cases declared "that verdicts should be set aside only in exceptional situations"[64] or where "the ends of justice would not be met by allowing . . . [them] to stand."[65] Especially when "the credibility of the witnesses [was] to be determined, the jury [was] supreme, and its verdict should not be overturned."[66]

New York judges did grant new trials, however, under some circumstances. New trials were granted or verdicts otherwise set aside, for example, in cases in which jury verdicts rested on legal theories that were contrary to law[67] or were completely without support in the evidence.[68] One such case was properly decided under the law existing at the time of the decision, but when the statute on which that law was based was subsequently declared unconstitutional by the Supreme Court of the United States, a new trial was granted "in furtherance of justice."[69]

Jury compromises constituted a common circumstance in which new trials were granted. In one breach of contract case, for example, a plaintiff was entitled to damages of $224.80 if the contract was as he alleged; when the jury returned a verdict for $100, the court found that the verdict was "manifestly the result of a compromise," and it granted a new trial.[70] Another verdict was set aside when the court concluded "from the facts, that the jury could not have agreed upon so insignificant a sum, as their award of damages to the plaintiff, without the sacrifice of principle ... [and] a compromise of the most objectionable type."[71]

Misconduct by either the trial judge[72] or trial counsel[73] was yet another reason for granting a new trial. New trials also were granted on the ground of newly discovered evidence.[74] Finally there were occasional cases in which new trials were granted because verdicts were contrary to the weight of the evidence,[75] as in one case involving a plaintiff's verdict for the death of a four-year-old boy in which the plaintiff's evidence was thin and the trial judge may have "believe[d] that the jury had not given the case the calm, impartial, unsympathetic consideration which was demanded."[76]

Summary

Despite the obvious pro-business orientation of judges in the last cited case, the evidence does not support a conclusion that the orientation of New York's law of procedure in the period from 1860 to 1920 was generally conservative in a pro-business sense. It is uncertain what interests benefitted from the replacement of the common law forms of action by a single cause of action or by the merger of law and equity. Since we cannot know whether defendants on average were likely to be more or less wealthy than plaintiffs, it is also uncertain whether the rich or the poor obtained greater benefit from the expanded ability of defendants to bring counterclaims under the Field Code. The poor were the beneficiaries of the 1831 legislation ending imprisonment for debt, but it is unclear who gained the benefit of the judiciary's interpretation of the law allowing imprisonment of those accused of negligence or fraud. As was shown in chapter 4, protecting the fact-finding power of juries most likely helped victims of personal injury, who typically had less wealth than the perpetrators of injury. Much about the law of procedure thus assisted society's "little fellows," but there was no overarching pattern that made that law genuinely progressive.

Conservatism and progressivism simply were not at the center of judges' minds. In regard to the law of procedure, judges cared about other values. Two opinions will illustrate.

Gnecco v. Pederson[77] articulated the judiciary's concern for the timely and efficient processing of litigation. The case involved a jury verdict in favor of a plaintiff who had been struck and injured by a defendant's automobile. Three juries had returned verdicts for plaintiff in amounts between $2,000 and $3,250, but all three verdicts had been set aside. On a fourth trial, the jury returned a verdict for $400, and both parties moved to set it aside and proceed to a fifth trial. The trial judge refused. He wrote:

> The prime object which courts should keep in view is the determination of controversies. This is what they are organized for, not to prolong strife nor inspire a litigious spirit. To attain this object, they should constantly strive on the one hand, not to become lax in the enforcement of legal rights, and on the other not to permit subtlety and technicality to frustrate the very right of the matter. It is an axiom that justice never tires, but it is equally true that justice deferred frequently becomes injustice. It is time this wasteful litigation was at an end. It has occupied the attention of the courts quite long enough.[78]

In addition to efficiency, courts were concerned about fairness. *Gould v. Cayuga County National Bank*[79] arose out of a plaintiff's suit to recover U.S. bonds that he had loaned to the bank, which the bank claimed it had returned. Before the suit was commenced, the parties agreed to a $25,000 settlement, which the bank paid in full satisfaction. Plaintiff then sued the bank, the bank pleaded the settlement in bar, but the plaintiff proved that the settlement had been procured by fraud. The court nonetheless upheld the settlement as a bar to the suit, ruling that the plaintiff had had to rescind the compromise before commencing suit. It gave the following hypothetical to illustrate its reasoning:

> Suppose A. goes abroad, leaving in the hands of his agent debts to be collected, against various debtors, among whom is B., a debtor for $1,000, and before his return his agent dies. Upon his return, he finds among his papers no evidence that B. paid his agent, and then he calls upon B. and he claims that he paid the agent the whole debt. A. disputes this and they finally agree to compromise the dispute, B. paying $500. Afterward A. concludes that B. did not in fact pay his agent and claims that he was induced, by fraud, to enter into the compromise. So long as the compromise remains in force, no action upon the original indebtedness can be maintained. The bar can be removed only by rescinding the compromise agreement, and that can be rescinded only by a restoration of the $500, so that they can resume their dispute upon a footing of equality.... When A. sues upon the original indebtedness, B. must be permitted to renew his dispute and set up payment of the entire debt to A.s agent. If he can establish that, the $500 will be again in his hands where it belongs. If he fails, A. will recover his whole debt. If A. can maintain his suit without first returning the $500, he will have all the game in his own hands. If he wins the suit he will retain the $500 and get $500 more. If he loses the suit in consequence of proof that the whole debt had been paid to his agent he will still have the $500. He will thus in effect hold B. to the compromise but himself be released. Such inequality and injustice cannot be tolerated by correct principles of law.[80]

The court did not care whether A or B was the wealthier of the two. It cared only that both be treated fairly, that A not receive more than he was owed, and that B not be made to pay more than he was indebted.

It was these concerns for efficiency and fairness in the adjudication of disputes, not the making of law on behalf of interest groups, that dominated judicial thinking in the 1860–1920 period. Especially in connection with the law of procedure, judges also were concerned that practices that had worked well in the past, such as the rules of common law pleading, not be cast aside without first being replaced by more workable, explicit, new rules.

6

The Law of Nuisance

New York's law of nuisance, as articulated by the court of appeals, was deeply precedent-oriented, anti-business and antidevelopment, and supportive of maintaining agricultural and residential neighborhoods. The policy of the court of appeals was to maintain neighborhoods as they existed unless entrepreneurs seeking to change the neighborhoods paid enough money to residents to obtain their consent to change.

An early case protected a country estate of some thirty to forty acres planted with ornamental trees and gardens. The neighborhood was largely agricultural until two years before the plaintiff brought suit, when the defendant opened a brick kiln 567 feet south of the plaintiff's estate. By using anthracite coal in the kiln, the defendant could produce 3,000,000 to 4,000,000 bricks annually at a good profit, but the anthracite also produced sulfurous acid gas that killed a total of $500 worth of the plaintiff's trees when the wind blew from the south, which it did on many occasions. On these facts the court of appeals affirmed an award of damages and a grant of injunctive relief, forcing the defendant to relocate his kiln and thereby preserve the residential character of the neighborhood.[1]

A second case involved a house on East Forty-Sixth Street in Manhattan of a value of at least $20,000, which a woman named Elizabeth Cogswell had purchased in 1870. Two years later, the New Haven Railroad bought the adjacent lot and built an engine house and coal bins for eleven engines. The engine house thereafter emitted offensive gases, smoke, soot, cinders, and coal dust that rendered the plaintiff's house uncomfortable and unhealthy. The court of appeals remanded the case for an award of injunctive relief and to determine the amount of damages.[2] Given the proximity of the engine house to the terminus of the railroad at Forty-Second Street, the railroad probably had to pay Ms. Cogswell and perhaps several other homeowners as well substantial sums of money to transform a residential block into a block appropriate for the railroad's needs.

A few years later, a homeowner located near a mill pond sued the Spencer Optical Manufacturing Co., which drew water from the pond as its power source. After the company's factory burned down, it build a new and apparently larger factory "at great expense" that drew more water from the pond, lowered the water level, and created a swampy area near the plaintiff's house that produced offensive odors and caused illnesses in the plaintiff's family. Again the court of appeals granted injunctive relief forcing the defendant either to move its factory or pay a substantial amount of money to the plaintiff so as to keep its factory running.[3]

The next case focused explicitly on the economic consequences of preserving a residential neighborhood. In that case, a gas company had functioned next to a homeowner for twenty years without difficulty. But in 1880, "for the sake of economy"—that is, to make greater profits—the company began using naphtha instead of coal to produce its gas, and the new production method produced offensive odors that made living in the plaintiff's house disagreeable. Again the court upheld an award of damages and a grant of injunctive relief that forced the gas company either to employ a less profitable mode of manufacturing gas or to give the plaintiff a payoff.[4]

The court of appeals was explicit about the issue of profits in an early-twentieth-century case, *McCarty v. Natural Carbonic Gas Co.*,[5] in which a manufacturer of carbonic acid gas emitted thick black smoke from two factory chimneys located less than one thousand feet from the plaintiff's house, which was "situated in a country district suitable for country homes."[6] The smoke resulted from the use of soft coal, in regard to which the court noted:

> all damage can be avoided by the use of hard coal, as is done by one of its competitors in the same kind of business in the same locality, or possibly by the use of some modern appliance such as a smoke consumer, although either would involve an increase in expense. It is better, however, that profits should be somewhat reduced than to compel a householder to abandon his home, especially when he did not come to the nuisance, but was there before.[7]

Accordingly, the court granted injunctive relief.

A final case, *Whalen v. Union Bag & Paper Co.*,[8] became a leading one. The company had spent more than a million dollars building a factory that employed four to five hundred workers and discharged into a creek pollution that caused a downstream farmer $312 in damages per year. Because "of the great loss likely to be inflicted on the defendant by the granting of the injunction as compared to the small injury done to the plaintiff's land,"[9] the Appellate Division reversed the trial court's grant of injunctive relief. The court of appeals, in turn, reversed the Appellate Division, stating that the intermediate court's rule was

> not a good reason for refusing an injunction. Neither courts of equity nor law can be guided by such a rule, for if fol-

lowed to its logical conclusion it would deprive the poor litigant of his little property by giving it to those already rich. It is always to be remembered in such cases that denying the injunction puts the hardship on the party in whose favor the legal right exists instead of on the wrongdoer. . . . Before locating the plant the owners were bound to know . . . [that] the magnitude of their investment and their freedom from malice furnish[ed] no reason why they should escape the consequences of their own folly.[10]

The court of appeals' preference in *Whalen* and *McCarty* for the "little fellow," for the country homeowner, and for the protection of agriculture was clear: the court understood that corporate entrepreneurs had money, and the court forced them, if they sought to change the character of a neighborhood, to redistribute some of that money to ordinary people whose well-being depended on the neighborhood's preservation.[11] In one important area, however, the court did take a different approach: it was unwilling to enjoin plans of improvement adopted in good faith by the state or by municipal governments[12] or by the federal government.[13]

Nonetheless the principal limitation on the court of appeals' preference for preserving neighborhoods and protecting "little fellows" lay in the discretion possessed by lower court judges. Lower court judges had discretion to grant or refuse equitable relief, and the court of appeals would not interfere lightly with their exercise of that discretion.[14] More importantly,

the law relating to private nuisances [was] a law of degree and usually turn[ed] on the question of fact whether the use [was] reasonable or not under all the circumstances. No hard and fast rule control[led] the subject, for a use that [was] reasonable under one set of facts would be unreasonable under another. . . . Whether the use of property by one person [was] reasonable, with reference to the comfortable

enjoyment of his own property by another, generally de-
pend[ed] upon many and varied facts; such as location, nature of the use, character of the neighborhood, extent and
frequency of the injury, the effect on the enjoyment of life,
health and property and the like.[15]

Lower court judges, often with the assistance of juries, thus possessed significant discretion in resolving such matters of fact. In
so doing, many of them faithfully enforced the policy preferences
of the court of appeals, but some took a more pro-entrepreneur-
ial, pro-business approach.

Cases in which lower courts granted remedies to plaintiffs often were strikingly similar to cases in the court of appeals. Courts,
for example, enjoined the maintenance of stables[16] and railroad
coal yards[17] in residential neighborhoods as well as manufacturing activities that produced smoke, gas, vibrations, or noise.[18]
They granted damages for injuries caused by explosions of dyna-
mite improperly stored in cities.[19] They granted damages against
a gaslight company that manufactured gas in a residential neighborhood[20] and enjoined similarly located electric companies,[21]
although a court granted one such company time to relocate its
plant in view of the inconvenience that would result to the public
from an immediate shutdown.[22] Finally, lower courts enjoined
activities that were lawful if properly conducted but became nuisances when conducted improperly,[23] or they granted damages to
those injured thereby.[24]

Other cases, in contrast, found that nearly identical land uses
did not constitute nuisances. There were cases, for example, finding that stables,[25] a railroad roundhouse,[26] a factory for polishing
marble,[27] another for making artificial ice,[28] and three cement
plants,[29] the storage of explosives,[30] the escape and explosion of
naphtha[31] and gasoline,[32] and pollution by power plants[33] were
not nuisances. Other cases in which nuisances were not found
involved a billboard,[34] a restaurant in a neighborhood zoned for

residences,[35] a hotel driveway used for delivery of supplies,[36] and a blacksmith shop.[37] Finally, courts did not find nuisances in the demolition of a building,[38] in the falling of an apartment house ceiling,[39] in the bursting of a fly wheel that killed a bystander,[40] in the construction of a building that could be rented to an industry that might become a nuisance in the future but was not yet occupied,[41] or in the maintenance of a metal cellar door on which a pedestrian slipped in a rainstorm.[42]

Probably the most important way in which lower courts failed to enforce the antidevelopment, anti-business policies of the court of appeals occurred in the many cases in which judges used their discretion to deny injunctions and to remit plaintiffs to their damage remedies at law.[43] These decisions were important because they significantly reduced the bargaining power of victims of nuisances. When those victims received injunctive relief, they could bargain with nuisance-creating entrepreneurs and force them either to cease their operations or to disgorge a portion of their profits. But when they could obtain only legal relief, they had no power to bargain and could recover only a damage award that was typically tiny in comparison with the profits of the entrepreneur.

The variability of nuisance law, as applied in the lower courts, is demonstrated by three hospital cases. In *Gilford v. Babies Hospital*,[44] the court granted an injunction to a neighboring resident against the construction of "a hospital for the care of sick infants, including any who . . . [might] develop, after admission, contagious disease." The court reached its result because it concluded that "the care of sick infants . . . [brought] danger to the youthful members of families living near" and "multiplie[d] the risk of ordinary existence, whatever may be the degree of care taken."[45] A quarter of a century later, *Hall v. House of St. Giles the Cripple*[46] denied similar relief to a neighbor of a hospital. It recognized that "the coming and going of crippled children . . . undoubtedly [would cause] pain and distress . . . to those living nearby simply

by having to observe suffering"[47] but nonetheless ruled that the
hospital was not a nuisance. Between the two cases, the Appellate
Division decided *Heaton v. Packer*,[48] which refused to enjoin the
construction of a hospital for the insane. Although the plaintiffs complained that the hospital would "make it dangerous for
women and children to go upon the streets . . . and make the residents nervous and ill from seeing unseemly sights and hearing
unseemly noises," the court concluded that, while "the establishment of a lunatic asylum in the plaintiffs neighborhood . . . [was]
not . . . a desirable thing still the evils apprehended do not necessarily arise from its maintenance, and are not inherent to it."[49]
Whatever one might think of the results in these three cases,
what seems clear is that the reasoning of the courts did not set
any clear standard about when it was appropriate to locate hospitals in residential neighborhoods. Everything was decided on a
case-by-case basis with judges free to resolve cases as they interpreted the facts and used their discretion.

Thus, in nuisance law, as in other bodies of doctrine, there was
tension between doing what was needed to develop the state, its
economy, and its well-being, on the one hand, and being fair to
individual litigants, especially to the less well-off and less fortunate inhabitants of the state, on the other. Appellate judges
typically favored established property holders such as farmers
and home owners, but trial judges sometimes exercised their
fact-finding and remedial discretion to assist business entrepreneurs. As a result, the law in the end left much decision-making
to the fact-finding and discretionary decision-making of juries
and judges in the lower courts. The result was neither a totally
conservative nor a totally progressive body of nuisance law but
something in between.

7

Religion and Morality

The part of New York law that was the most backward-looking, with almost no input of progressivism, was the law dealing with religion and with the moral precepts associated with religion. This conservatism had nothing to do, however, with favoring the interests of the rich. Instead, it was about keeping entrenched traditional Christian values that dated back centuries.

An early case made this clear, when a justice of the New York Supreme Court declared:

> It is not disputed that Christianity is a part of the common law of England, . . . and ever has been, a part of the law of the state. . . . It would be strange that a people, Christian in doctrine and worship, . . . who regarded religion as the basis of their civil liberty, and the foundation of their rights, should, in their zeal to secure to all the freedom of conscience which they valued so highly, solemnly repudiate and put beyond the pale of the law, the religion which was dear to them as life, and dethrone the God who . . . had been their protector and guide as a people.[1]

Keeping Holy the Lord's Day

The first way in which New York courts kept Christianity a part of the state's law was by making the "observance of Sunday," the Christian sabbath, "to some extent compulsory, not by way of enforcing the conscience of those upon whom the law operates, but by way of protection to those who desire and are entitled to the day."[2] "The right to rear a family with a becoming regard to the institutions of christianity, and . . . a decent observance of the sabbath" was "as much the subject of government protection as any other right of person or property."[3] Protection of this right accordingly made "the christian sabbath . . . one of the civil institutions of the state . . . to which the business and duties of life are, by the common law, made to conform and adapt themselves."[4]

Doing business on Sunday was prohibited, and when Jewish merchants sought to stay open on Sunday, pointing out that they celebrated the sabbath on Saturday and closed their store that day, they were denied the injunctive relief they sought.[5] Similarly, a New York judge refused to give approval to the certificate of formation of a Jewish membership corporation that planned to meet on Sundays. He inferred

from the face of the certificate before me that the members of the proposed corporation are of a race and religion by which not the first, but the seventh, day of the week, is set apart for religious observance. The fact might be of decisive importance were a desecration of their holy day contemplated; but the act intended is an aggression upon the Christian Sabbath. The law which scrupulously protects them in the observance of their ceremonial gives them no license, as I am sure they have no desire, to affront the religious susceptibilities of others.[6]

New York law also rejected the claim that citizens had a right "to regard the sabbath as a day of recreation and amusement, rather than as a day of rest and religious worship."[7] For that reason, the courts upheld convictions for exhibiting a dramatic performance on Sunday,[8] for fishing on Sunday,[9] and as late as 1917 for playing baseball on Sunday, even when the proceeds of the game were paid to a charity for the relief of war suffering.[10]

Upholding Religious Leaders

The second way in which New York courts supported religion was by upholding the jurisdiction of duly constituted religious authorities to govern and administer their churches. Judges declared "that all questions of faith, doctrine, and discipline belong[ed] exclusively to the church and its spiritual officers" and therefore refused to interfere in such matters.[11] Duly constituted religious authorities thus governed the appointment, support, and removal of clergymen.[12] In *Baxter v. McDonnell*,[13] for example, where a Roman Catholic priest sought to sue his bishop for his salary, the court of appeals rejected the suit. The court held that the relation between priest and bishop was

> in no sense that of master and servant, but that of an ecclesiastical superior and inferior, with an alleged obligation arising from the laws of the church. . . . It would be doing a wrong to the Catholic church and degrade its priesthood from their high position were we to hold that the relation between the bishop and his priest was that of hirer and hired, of employer and employee. . . . When a priest dedicates his life to the church and takes upon himself the vows of obedience to its laws, he is presumed to be actuated by a higher principle than the hope of gain. . . . Where he relies

upon the duty of his church to support him, he must invoke the aid of the church if he seeks redress."[14]

Religious authorities also set standards for church membership,[15] controlled church property,[16] could close a church over the objection of its congregation,[17] and possessed the power to sue and be sued in the name of the church.[18] Unless property had been given to a church as a member of a specific denomination,[19] early cases even gave controlling local religious authorities the power to change the denomination to which a local church belonged.[20] Legislation of 1875[21] and 1876,[22] however, deprived them of that power and required them to administer the property of local congregations in accordance with the rules and usages of whatever denomination, if any, to which a local congregation belonged.[23]

Courts did have some capacity to monitor the fairness of elections of church officials, but even in cases challenging elections, judges tended to defer to church rules and usages.[24] In *Lynch v. Pfeiffer*,[25] for example, in which a meeting that organized a church consisted only of male members and elected only male officers, the court rejected a claim that the meeting was illegally organized because women were also entitled to vote. The court of appeals responded to the claim as follows:

> If we assume that all members of the congregation of lawful age had the right to participate in the meeting, it is not shown that any were excluded. While it is recited in the certificate that the meeting was composed of the male members of the society, for aught that appears the female members may have absented themselves, and if they did the male members had the right to constitute the meeting. Certainly there is nothing to show that any female member was excluded from the meeting.[26]

Lynch v. Pfeiffer, as much as anything, illustrates the character of turn-of-the-century judicial conservatism. Conservatism was not about favoring people of wealth but about preserving the existing order. Some churches were ordered hierarchically; others were subject to more local, democratic control. Courts protected the power structures of both sorts of churches. What courts opposed was radical dissidents seeking fundamental social change, such as priests suing their bishops for salaries or women who by demanding a right to vote threatened long-standing male hegemony. Late nineteenth-century judges had witnessed earlier radicals, both antislavery and proslavery, tear the nation apart, and they were not ready to give assistance to any new forms of radicalism.

Enforcing Norms of Sexuality and Marriage

The third way in which turn-of-the-century New York law supported religion was by enforcing traditional Christian moral values: "Christianity . . . [was] the basis of public morals."[27] As one New York judge declared, the Christian religion was "intimately connected with a good government, and the only sure basis of sound morals"; it "furnish[ed] the best sanctions of moral and social obligations."[28] It was, in his view, "the right of every citizen to be protected from offenses against decency, and against acts which tend to corrupt the morals and debase the moral sense of the community."[29] Enforcement of traditional Christian values protected the people from "blasphemy, sabbath-breaking, incest, polygamy and the like,"[30] as well as crimes of prostitution,[31] abortion,[32] and homosexuality, the nature of which "forbids our dwelling upon the facts."[33] Another crime was indecent exposure, in one case of which six women exposed themselves, for money, in an "indescribably indecent" fashion for five men who watched them in the back room of a house of prostitution.[34]

INDECENCY

The crimes just mentioned generated few judicial opinions, but another crime of immorality—indecency—generated several. An outrageous, deeply conservative case was *People v. Byrne*,[35] in which Ethel Byrne was charged with disseminating condoms along with

> literature dealing with the question of conception and setting forth various ways and means by which it could be prevented. One of these pamphlets is labeled "What Every Girl Should Know." This contains matters which not only should not be known by every girl, but perhaps should not be known by any. The distribution of these pamphlets, especially to girls just coming into womanhood, would be a shocking disgrace to the community.[36]

Byrne was found guilty and given a prison sentence despite her claim that the legislation under which she was prosecuted was unconstitutional. The court rejected that claim, noting that "men and women and boys and girls lacking in moral stamina are deterred from fornication by the fear of . . . pregnancy." It continued that "fornication . . . surely offends the moral sense of a large portion of the people of this state" and that "the Legislature has a right to declare . . . acts illegal which are in conflict with the moral sense of the people." In something of a non sequitur, the court added that the legislature also "has the power to declare that articles should not be used to prevent conception of married women."[37] Later the court said:

> The literature distributed by the defendant is as harmful as the use of the articles sold. The book, entitled "What Every Girl Should Know," is especially objectionable. It contains pictures of certain organs of a woman. . . . The distribution

of this book and diffusion of knowledge of its contents, especially among girls and boys coming into the period of adolescence, would produce most harmful results. The information would make people generally believe that by using the means suggested the act of intercourse could be had without the fear of resulting pregnancy. . . . To remove that fear would unquestionably result in an increase of immorality.[38]

Another case[39] involved a conviction for a theatrical performance of a pantomime about a bride and bridegroom on the night of their wedding. After he takes her to a bed, she leads him out of the room, although he indicates he will be back in five minutes. She then undresses, although "she dexterously limits the exposure of her person," and gets into bed. Then there is a knock at the door, she says "Entrez, and the curtain falls."[40] The court found this performance "really more dangerous to public morals than any mere vulgar exhibition of nudity. The latter may arouse impure thoughts, but it is more apt to excite disgust." The court expressed its concern about "an appeal to the imagination," noting that "when the suggestion is immoral, the more that is left to the imagination the more subtle and seductive the influence." The court concluded that the defendant's aim "was not to honor, but to degrade marriage; and the defendant's guilt [was] enhanced, not diminished, by his utilization of its sacred confidences to serve his criminal purpose."[41]

A third case, *People v. Muller*,[42] which was decided by the court of appeals, was a prosecution of an art dealer for selling photographic reproductions of nude paintings that had been exhibited at the Salon in Paris and the Centennial Exhibition in Philadelphia. The court recognized that "mere nudity in painting or sculpture is not obscenity. . . . It [was] a false delicacy and mere prudery which would . . . banish from sight all such objects." The "test of obscenity or indecency in a picture or statue [was] whether it [was] naturally calculated to excite in a spectator impure imaginations." That was a question of fact for the jury. In the court's view, it did "not require an expert in art or literature to determine whether a picture [was] obscene or whether printed words [were] offensive to decency"; these were "matters which f[e]ll within the range of ordinary intelligence,"[43] and since the jury in *Muller* had found the photographs obscene, the court affirmed the defendant's conviction.

Limits existed, however, to the willingness of courts to uphold indecency convictions. In a case in which a defendant was prosecuted for saying in Polish about an identified woman, "She is a whore," the court of appeals concluded that the defendant was not guilty of an act that outraged public decency and therefore reversed his conviction. The court noted that the woman could sue the defendant for slander, but that slander was only a tort, not a crime. It also noted that the defendant, a leader of a labor strike, had spoken at a labor meeting at which the woman had urged a return to work. In that context, as distinguished from a context of, say, a woman's luncheon at a country club, the words arguably were not seriously offensive.[44] In two other cases, courts held that living with a man as his wife and assuming his surname when he was married to another woman[45] and that an invitation by a married man to a married woman to "meet each other for a good time"[46] did not constitute criminal behavior. Courts finally aided defendants procedurally by requiring indictments to provide at least a general description of allegedly indecent matter,[47] although one court held it sufficient to give the title of an obscene book and state that "the obscene matter . . . [was] so gross as to be . . . improper to be placed upon its [the court's] records."[48]

The most telling limitation on prosecutions for indecency occurred in *People v. Eastman*.[49] The publication said to be indecent in that case called "the confessional box" of the Roman Catholic Church "hell's gate . . . [and] the mainspring to lust." It continued:

Here the priest asks the vilest of questions. . . . He asks the most delicate and intimate questions. But under what obligation is any one to a priest? What business has he got to go into a box and ask delicate female questions that no minister of Jesus Christ or true gentleman on earth would ask? Right here in the confessional box many have been ruined, and many become mothers as a result; and men, you are paying your money to priests and to a church that is ruining your daughters and stealing the affections of your wife, until he knows more about her than you do. She has many secrets kept from you, husband, but not from that licentious priest.[50]

A per curiam opinion found this publication "improper, intemperate, unjustifiable, and highly reprehensible," but not "indecent as that word [was] employed . . . in the Penal Code."[51]

Indecency meant only obscenity, and something was obscene only if it excited sexual pleasure, not if it challenged a religious belief or reflected anger at a union meeting toward a woman taking the side of management. Courts in the indecency cases were not upholding the authority or prestige of religious leaders or any other leaders. Rather they were upholding the traditional Christian religious norm that rejected ancient concepts of sex as a form of pleasure and that confined sexual intercourse to married couples as an unfortunate but necessary precondition of procreation.

Marriage and Divorce

New York courts also defended traditional Christian values in regard to the law of marriage. "Marriage [was] more than a civil contract, which . . . the parties [might] break or terminate at will." It was "a *status*, which involve[d] the welfare of the public";[52] it was "the mother of purity and virtue and the guardian angel of the human race,"[53] all of which made the courts "always . . . very reluctant to disturb the sanctity of the marriage relation."[54] Thus they upheld common-law marriages,[55] especially in cases involving ceremonial marriages where some impediment had made the marriage invalid but where husband and wife continued to live together after the impediment to their marriage had been removed.[56] In *Geiger v. Ryan*,[57] for example, a justice of the peace in 1867 performed an invalid marriage of a man and a women who was already married to a first husband. But when the first husband died in 1885 and she continued to live as husband and wife with her 1867 second husband, that marriage became valid and on her death in 1903 he was held to be her widower.

Courts also upheld traditional values by granting divorce sparingly. Divorce a vinculo, which permitted a plaintiff to remarry, was available only on the ground of a spouse's adultery,[58] and a major issue in many divorce cases was the sufficiency of the evidence of alleged adultery. Adultery had to be proved by "clear and convincing evidence."[59] Thus the court of appeals held in a leading case that adultery could not be proved by the testimony of neighbors that they believed that a man was married to a woman who frequented his house and that he was engaging in sexual intercourse with her, when unbeknownst to the neighbors he was in fact married to another woman.[60] The same was true of testimony by a detective who bored two small holes in the door of a room in which, he claimed, he observed the defendant having sexual intercourse with companions,[61] of testimony that a female defendant spent five to ten minutes alone with her alleged paramour in his room,[62] and of evidence of "association, frequent interviews, and intimacy . . . but no credible evidence of improper conduct . . . or any criminal attachment."[63] One trial judge even rejected testimony by a witness that he committed adultery with one of the parties to a divorce suit; "the rule," according to the court, was "that the evidence of a man who is willing to swear away the reputation of a woman, with whom he claims to have had sexual intercourse, should be received with extreme caution, and only when corroborated by other proof."[64] On the other hand, courts did conclude that adultery had been committed in a case in which a husband had entered the room of an inmate of a brothel, remained for approximately an hour, and came out and handed a bill to the brothel's proprietress[65] and in a case in which a woman whose bedroom was located between the bedrooms of her husband and her alleged paramour bolted the door to her husband's bedroom and left the door to her paramour's room unfastened—a fact that the court called "very suggestive."[66]

Spouses unable to obtain a divorce a vinculo often sought to terminate their marriages by getting them annulled, but courts were equally sparing in granting annulments. Annulments were granted on the ground of duress, as when a woman falsely accused a man of being the father of her child in order to force him into marriage.[67] Annulments were also granted for fraud, such as the concealment of a material fact like a venereal disease,[68] tuberculosis,[69] insanity,[70] or pregnancy.[71] Marriages also could be annulled if one of the parties was married[72] or underage[73] at the time of the marriage, but courts sometimes refused to annul them.[74] Courts also refused to grant annulments to a woman who married a sixty-nine-year-old man plagued with "physical incapacity,"[75] to a man who married a woman incapable of bearing children,[76] to another man who married a woman whose vagina was "short[er] . . . than the average, [but] still . . . within normal lengths,"[77] and to a third man who married a woman who previously had given birth to an illegitimate child.[78]

To preserve its law that divorce a vinculo was available only on the ground of adultery, as well as its practice of limiting grants of annulment, New York courts typically declined to recognize out-of-state divorces unless both parties had actual notice of and had actually appeared in the out-of-state proceeding.[79] As a result, one man who remarried in reliance on an Ohio divorce decree was prosecuted for and convicted of bigamy.[80] Facts, however, could become quite complicated. In *Peugnet v. Phelps*,[81] a husband had divorced his wife for adultery pursuant to a decree that prohibited her from remarrying until that husband's death. She then went across the Hudson River to Jersey City, where she married the man with whom she had committed the adultery. Subsequently that man sought an annulment of the marriage on the ground that she lacked the capacity to marry him because of the prohibition on her remarriage. The New York court held that it did not have jurisdiction to annul an out-of-state marriage, while noting, however, that the woman might be subject to "punishment . . . for disobeying the command of the court."[82]

A divorce a mensa et thoro—that is, a decree of separation that did not permit remarriage—could be obtained on lesser grounds either of abandonment or of cruelty. Abandonment consisted of "absence . . . coupled with an intent not to return."[83] In addition to a remedy for support against a departing spouse,[84] an innocent spouse might also have a suit for alienation of affections against a third party who encouraged or assisted an abandonment.[85] Abandonment, however, was sometimes "justified" if the spouse who was deserted "did much to foment difficulty," and in such cases would not be a basis for a separation decree. The fact, however, "that a wife [was] so temperamentally constituted as to be nervous and hysterical . . . [were] reasons for care and commiseration [rather] than for an abandonment."[86]

As for cruelty, black-letter law required "either . . . actual violence or a reasonable apprehension of bodily injury. . . . Occasional outbursts of passion [would] not do," but "words of menace would be sufficient if they be of such a character . . . as to justify a belief in their seriousness."[87] Some courts, however, went further, holding that physical violence or the threat thereof were not necessary and that "conduct and language which cause great mental suffering, and which are persisted in, . . . [could] be the basis of a separation."[88] Repeated accusations of adultery, made without grounds for believing it to be true, were an example.[89] Other examples of nonphysical cruelty were abusive treatment by a mother-in-law in which a husband acquiesced,[90] compelling a wife to undergo abortions,[91] or having a venereal disease.[92] Cruelty by one spouse would not be a basis for separation, however, if it resulted from bad conduct by the other.[93]

An important issue in divorce and separation cases was custody of children. Courts, motivated by regard for the best interests of children, typically gave custody, particularly of younger children, to their mothers,[94] even when those mothers remarried after receiving an out-of-state divorce that was not recognized by New York and thus were technically guilty of adultery against the child's father.[95] Courts would not remove a child from its mother's custody even if custody by the father became more advantageous for the child when such removal would have a negative impact on the child's education.[96] Courts would give custody to a father, however, when a divorce or separation resulted from a mother's abandonment of the family.[97]

Another important issue was financial support. In this regard, courts generally behaved conservatively in adhering to the traditional Christian view that men were obligated to support the women they married and the children they fathered.[98] But there were limits to what courts were willing to provide. As one court explained, a "judgment of separation did not dissolve the marriage relation. That relation still continued with all the legal obligations of the husband to provide for the support of the wife." In cases of absolute divorce, however, alimony was "in the nature of a penalty imposed upon the guilty party for a violation of his marriage vows and obligations"—"a substitute for the rights of the innocent wife." Thus, when a woman obtained an out-of-state absolute divorce without obtaining an award of alimony in the divorce decree, she lost any claim for support.[99] A woman also lost her right of support from a divorced husband when she remarried a new husband capable of supporting her, although the divorced husband still was required to support his minor children.[100] It finally must be noted that support was not always generous: one court, for example, found an award of one-third of a man's income for both wife and children excessive.[101]

In connection with marriages that remained intact, courts routinely gave effect to statutory mandates of 1848,[102] 1849,[103] and 1860[104] permitting married women to function independently of their husbands. But in the absence of legislation, judges behaved conservatively by keeping women in the common law's position of subordination.

By the 1870s, there could "be no longer a question that a married woman [could] carry on business on her sole and separate account, and that in such business she [could] purchase property for cash or upon credit."[105] A married woman could hold legal title to the rents and profits of her real estate as against her husband and his creditors,[106] as well as to any earnings from services rendered to third parties.[107] Property given by a husband to his wife for use in her separate business also belonged to the wife,[108] as did her personal property lent to her husband for use in his business.[109] A married woman could even employ her husband as her agent to run her business,[110] or could act on his behalf under a secret trust.[111] Of course, a married woman was also liable for her separate debts,[112] including any arising out of her rental of real estate that constituted her and her husband's home.[113]

But the legislation of 1848, 1849, and 1860 did not

absolve a married woman from the duties which she owes to her husband, to render him service in his household, to care for him and their common children with dutiful affection when he or they need her care, and to render all the services in her household which are commonly expected of a married woman, according to her station in life. Nor was it the purpose of the statute[s] to absolve her from due obedience and submission to her husband as head and master of his household. . . . He is to determine where he and his family shall have a domicile, how his household shall be regulated and managed, and who shall be members of his family. . . . It would operate disastrously upon domestic life and breed discord and mischief if the wife could contract with her husband for . . . compensation for services, disagreeable or otherwise, rendered to members of his family. . . . To allow such contracts would degrade the wife by making her a menial and a servant in the home where she should discharge marital duties in loving and devoted ministrations.[114]

Accordingly, the court of appeals held that a husband and wife could not make a contract for her to be paid to care for his elderly mother who was living in their home.

The court also gave a narrow construction to the legislation, allowing married women to engage in business separate from their husbands. It ruled that the legislation permitted a married woman to

elect to labor on her own account, and thereby entitle herself to her earnings, but in the absence of such an election or of circumstances showing that she intended to avail herself of the privilege and protection conferred by the statute[s], the husband's common law right to her earnings remained unaffected. . . . Where the husband and wife are living together, and mutually engaged in providing for the support of themselves and their family,—each contributing by his or her labor to the promotion of the common purpose—and there is nothing to indicate an intention on the part of the wife to separate her earnings from those of her husband, her earnings, in that case, belong, we think, as at common law, to the husband.[115]

Thus, a husband was held entitled to compensation due for his wife's services to a boarder in their house who became ill.[116] On a similar presumption that husbands and wives acted in concert for the well-being of their families, a wife was presumed to be acting as her husband's agent in purchasing necessaries for the household[117] or authorizing work on the house itself.[118]

In short, much of the law dealing with sexuality and marriage conservatively remained what it had been for centuries. Judges did honor the statutorily created right of married women, who demanded the right, to function in a fashion economically independent of their husbands. Contrary to the traditional common-law rule, women who obtained divorces typically received custody of their children as well as financial support, however ungenerous that support often might have been. Otherwise the law remained what it had long been. The law sought to keep sexual activity and reference to it hidden in the recesses of the marital bedroom. Full divorce permitting remarriage was available in New York only for adultery, and separation, without the right to remarry, only for the narrow categories of abandonment and cruelty. Above all, when women did not act explicitly to demand their economic independence, the law assumed they remained under their husband's economic control, and it gave their husbands effective ownership of their property and earnings. Husbands remained as well the masters of their households, and wives owed them dutiful and loving service.

In conjunction with the laws protecting the Sabbath and upholding the authority of religious leaders, the law dealing with sexuality and marriage was deeply conservative. A person coming in a time machine from sixteenth-century Reformation England to turn-of-the-century New York would have found the law of religion and morality and the social practices associated with it largely familiar. A person from the twenty-first century, in contrast, who sought to live in early-twentieth-century New York by twenty-first-century norms would quickly find herself fined or even imprisoned. Turn-of-the-century New York remained very much a site of male hegemony.

Conclusion
THE EMERGENCE OF POLICY-ORIENTED JUDGING

Was New York law in the late nineteenth and early twentieth centuries conservative? The answer depends on the meaning of conservatism. The cases discussed in the previous chapters establish beyond doubt that if conservatism is defined as a pattern of consistent judicial decision-making in favor of big business and people of wealth, New York law was not conservative. On the contrary, the most important impact of the sixty-year period of adjudication between 1860 and 1920 was to lay the foundation for the twentieth-century regulatory state put into place by Governors Alfred E. Smith, Franklin D. Roosevelt, and Herbert Lehman.

But New York judges did adapt an approach to law that was profoundly conservative in two other respects. As has been shown, one form this conservatism took was to turn to history and precedent as a means of avoiding policy analysis and political choice. Another form was to turn to precedent and the past because the legal values of the early republic, whatever they were, were thought to be nobler and better than the profit-centered values of the late nineteenth century. Glimpses of this conservatism had appeared earlier, when, for example, Chief Justice John Marshall distinguished law from politics in *Marbury v. Madison*[1] and when numerous judges decided cases on the basis of precedent. But this conservatism developed fully and took root only in the post–Civil War era, when a powerful need emerged to avoid making new law on the basis of policy.

In fact, this adherence to precedent rested on two false premises. The first false premise was that the determination of judges to rely on precedent in order to avoid making policy judgments on a case-by-case basis reflected a fundamental political decision that judges should strive for societal harmony and stability rather than strive to seek right and to do justice. The second false premise was that earlier law in America had been apolitical; in fact, it had not been. Colonial judges, most of whom were not lawyers, often had been politically active partisans.[2] State-level judicial review cases during the 1780s similarly had resolved politically divisive issues.[3] In a deeply politicized fashion, Chief Justice Theophilus Parsons of Massachusetts, who as an appellate litigator had lost a series of cases in the 1780s dealing with the scope of the religious establishment's powers, overruled those 1780s cases he had lost in the 1810 case of *Barnes v. First Parish in Falmouth*,[4] which led, in turn, to the Religious Freedom Act of 1811 and to the case of *Adams v. Howe*,[5] which effectively overruled *Barnes*.[6] And, Chief Justice Marshall's successors, Roger Taney and Salmon P. Chase, as shown in the introduction, had not kept Marshall's promise to avoid political decision-making. More importantly, antebellum New York judges had not made a similar promise to stay out of politics or adopted a practice of doing so. In the decade before the Civil War, for instance, New York courts had passed on two divisive political issues—the constitutionality of legislation prohibiting the sale of alcoholic beverages[7] and the claimed right of slave owners to transport their slaves through New York.[8]

Despite these false premises, New York judges in the late nineteenth and early twentieth centuries nonetheless developed a conception of judging that strove to keep law distinct from and independent of politics and to generate a rule of law that transcended politics by avoiding policy making in deciding individual cases and turning to the readily available alternative of precedent and history—in particular to the history of the founding era and of the early republic, which they viewed as a time when judges had behaved apolitically. This recourse to precedent had the effect, of course, of keeping the law mired conservatively in the past and of antagonizing progressives who were seeking to have judges move the law forward—something they often had done earlier in the century by making progressive policy choices.

Because of judges' hostility to policy, the task that the courts in large part performed was dispute resolution, not lawmaking. Most disputes were resolved in the lower courts, where judges and juries had enormous fact-finding discretion that was rarely overturned and that made no law beyond that applicable to the case being decided. If the litigants raised more general questions of law, appellate judges would decide them, almost invariably on the basis of precedent or established societal principles, such as the free labor ideology of the antebellum era. Occasionally, as in contract law and corporate law, courts would establish necessary new rules, but they typically would do so inarticulately, without explaining why the new rules were necessary to meet society's needs. As I think back over the many cases discussed and cited in the preceding chapters, I can think of many that cited precedent or that explained how a court's decision was related to shared, existing norms of political morality. But I cannot think of any that explained analytically how some new rule was adopted to fulfill an emerging societal need.

Of course, judges understood that the opinions they published would provide guidance to future judges and lawyers. They understood, that is, that their guidance constituted law. They understood that law moved forward slowly by accretion but primarily in directions it had long been moving. They also understood that they did not possess power to alter the direction of the law's movement beyond what was unavoidable in response to new societal needs.

This apolitical, precedent-oriented conception of judging adopted in the interest of societal harmony and stability in aftermath of the Civil War endured, however, for only about one-third of a century, when it was challenged among other things by two pieces of writing, both authored by distinguished judges. The first appeared at the end of the nineteenth century and the second, at the close of the second decade of the twentieth. When we read these writings today, they simply describe what judges obviously do—they describe judicial policymaking that we take for granted. But only a few decades after the bloodiest war in American history, when most judges still remained committed to avoiding the sort of political decision-making that they understood had contributed to that war, the writings reflected a newly emerging, important point of view.

In 1897, Oliver Wendell Holmes, then a justice of the Supreme Judicial Court of Massachusetts, delivered a lecture to commemorate the opening of a new academic building at Boston University's School of Law. Titled "The Path of the Law,"[9] the lecture both described what Holmes understood judges did and set out a program for what they ought to do in the future. "The language of judicial decision," Holmes declared, was "mainly the language of logic," which "flatter[ed] that longing for certainty and repose which is in every human mind."[10] Underlying logic was history. Holmes explained that "if we want to know why a rule of law has taken its particular shape . . . or . . . why it exists at all, we go to tradition." "The rational study of law," he added, was "to a large extent the study of history."[11]

History and logic, however, were not the real forces dictating the substance of law. Behind history and logic, according to Holmes, was "a judgment as to the relative worth and importance of competing legislative grounds, often an inarticulate and unconscious judgment," but "the root and nerve of the whole proceeding—some opinion as to policy."[12] The main point of Holmes's lecture was to bring policy analysis into the open. Holmes thought it "revolting to have no better reason for a rule of law than that so it was laid down in the time of Henry IV,"[13] and he "look[ed] forward to a time when the part played by history in the explanation of dogma shall be very small, and instead of ingenious research we shall spend our energy on a study of the ends sought to be attained and the reasons for desiring them."[14]

At the close of the second decade of the twentieth century, Benjamin Cardozo, then a judge on the New York Court of Appeals, delivered the Storrs Lectures at Yale Law School, which he published in 1921 under the title, *The Nature of the Judicial Process*.[15] Cardozo was more willing than Holmes to follow precedent, but he agreed that "if the accepted rule . . . yield[ed] a result which [was] felt to be unjust, the rule [was] reconsidered." The rule might "not be modified at once, . . . but if a rule continue[d] to work injustice, it [would] eventually be reformulated."[16] For Cardozo as for Holmes, "not the origin, but the goal, [was] the main thing."[17] In a chapter titled "The Method of Sociology: The Judge as a Legislator,"[18] Cardozo wrote:

> My analysis of the judicial process comes then to this, and little more: logic, and history, and custom, and utility, and the accepted standards of right conduct, are the forces which singly or in combination shape the progress of the law. Which of these forces shall dominate in any case must depend largely upon the comparative importance or value of the social interests that will be thereby promoted or impaired. One of the most fundamental social interests is that law shall be uniform and impartial. . . . Therefore in the main there shall be adherence to precedent. . . . But symmetrical development may be bought at too high a price. Uniformity ceases to be a good when it becomes uniformity

of oppression. The social interest served by symmetry or certainty must then be balanced against the social interest served by equity and fairness or other elements of social welfare.[19]

This understanding led Cardozo to conclude, contrary to the predominant understanding of late-nineteenth-century New York judges, that "the law which is the resulting product [was] not found, but made."[20]

Many New York judges as late as 1920 did not agree with Holmes and Cardozo that judges should decide issues of policy in determining the outcome of cases. Many judges urged that the judicial process should remain apolitical and that issues of policy should be left to the legislature and to the people themselves. As a result of cases such as *Lochner v. New York*[21] and *McPherson v. Buick Motor Co.*,[22] lawyers today tend to think of Holmes and Cardozo as progressives and those who disagreed with them as conservatives. But we need finally to inquire whether those labels are right and, if they are right, in what sense judges who had an apolitical understanding of the judicial process were conservative.

We need to begin by inquiring whether policy-oriented decision-making is necessarily progressive. The answer is that it is not. Policy-oriented judges can be reactionary as well as progressive. Judges who are committed to deciding cases on the basis of logic and precedent may have a more progressive perspective than some politically oriented, reactionary judges. In particular, apolitical judges likely will be willing to accept progressive changes in the law enacted by the legislature, whereas reactionary judges may not.[23]

Next we need to focus on a particular hypothetical judge. Assume that a judge correctly understands that a progressive change that she favors will be opposed by a large number of people if it is imposed by the court on which she sits, will therefore be difficult to enforce, and may be overturned by a future court. She also understands that if politics is left to run its course, the public over time will come to support the change she favors, the legislature will enact it, and the new law, in the form in which it is enacted, will be more easily enforced and will more readily become a permanent part of the law. Accordingly she decides to vote against imposition of the change by her court.

Is this judge a progressive or a conservative? She understands that some people will remain under disadvantage for as long as change is postponed. That understanding points toward conservatism. But she also understands that change will take hold more readily if it is postponed until the public is prepared to allow the legislature to make it. That understanding points toward progressivism.

What if she is a judge with humility who does not know for sure whether the change she favors is socially desirable and does not know whether the public will accept it if it is imposed by her court? Does her humility make her a conservative? Or is judicial humility a positive trait that progressives should want judges to embrace?

I do not know whether to characterize this hypothetical judge as progressive or conservative, and I doubt whether the attachment of either label really matters. What I do know is that if this hypothetical judge is called a conservative, her conservatism is different from that of judges who favor big business and the wealthy and from that of judges who apply doctrines from the past because they believe that the law of the past is socially desirable.

As already noted, New York judges of the late nineteenth and early twentieth centuries were not conservative in the sense of favoring big business or the wealthy. Sometimes they did decide cases in favor of those interests, but that was not their general practice. More often the New York judiciary declined to make progressive changes in the law for reasons of institutional competence and deference to the political process. In *Ives v. South*

Buffalo Ry. Co.,[24] for example, the court of appeals concluded that New York's initial effort at workers' compensation was in conflict with the due process clauses of the federal and state constitutions. Although workers' compensation was a "reform ... devoutly to be wished"[25] for the many good reasons identified by the commission that had proposed the legislation, the court concluded that the need to modify its understanding of the requirements of due process in order to uphold the legislation constituted "an appeal which must be made to the people and not to the courts."[26] Thus, when the people amended the state constitution to authorize the enactment of workers' compensation, the court readily abandoned its federal constitutional concerns and upheld a new law's constitutionality.[27]

Even the judiciary's narrow reading of the Field Code, which insured that the common law and the fact-finding power of juries remained intact, may have occurred for reasons of institutional competence. Judges may have wanted simply to continue old common law practices, but they may also have been, as they claimed, unable to interpret the code except against the background of the common law and of jury power. New York judges, that is, may have been unwilling as a general matter to make "revolutionary"[28] changes in the law without a clear direction from the political process together with clear guidance about how to do so.

Thus, although it may not be incorrect to label the New York judiciary of the 1860–1920 era conservative, it is necessary to understand that the judicial conservatism of the late nineteenth and early twentieth centuries meant something different from what conservatism means today. Most New York judges between 1860 and 1920 appear to have understood that they lacked the jurisdiction and power to impose progressive social change that the political process was not prepared to enact. Some judges of that era also appear to have favored old law as a matter of desirable social policy. Judges today, in contrast, like colonial judges and judges of the antebellum years of the nineteenth century, do not appear especially deferential to the political process. Nor do they display great knowledge of or nostalgia for what old law in fact was.

Unlike New York judges of the late nineteenth and early twentieth centuries, who did not consistently favor big business and the rich, judges of today tend to support the interests of those who facilitated their ascension to the bench. Women, people of color, and others who ascend the bench with the support of reformers tend to support the progressive agendas of the groups of which they are a part. In opposition to these progressives, judges who come to the bench with the support of big business and people of wealth similarly tend to support those interests. Because they often oppose progressives, they call themselves "conservative." Thus they are like the conservatives of the 1860–1920 era in that they oppose progressivism. But the reasons for their opposition are different, and those reasons make their conservatism quite different indeed.

Why did today's conservatism develop differently from the conservatism of the late nineteenth century? The answer, I suggest, is that everyone today is a legal realist—every judge, that is, understands that policy choice lies at the foundation of judicial decision-making. Holmes, Cardozo, and their legal realist successors correctly understood the nature of the judicial process. Today's judges accordingly will often turn to policy in deciding cases—typically, to the policy values they held before ascending the bench. A widespread value among political conservatives is that an unregulated free market is economically superior to a regulated economy. When men and women who hold that view ascend the bench, they thus will become conservative judges who decide cases in a fashion enabling big business and the rich to maximize their wealth in an unregulated free market. How best to make society and the economy function, which is a matter of sharp political disagreement, rather than the maintenance of political and social stability lies at the root of much judicial decision-making.

Some people today will want to reestablish the judicial conservatism of a century ago. There is good reason for them to want to do so. Courts have limited power to enforce their judgments, and much of that power rests on the public's understanding that the judgments are neutral, objective, fair, and nonpolitical. Keeping the judiciary out of politics, as the old conservatism sought to do, thus would strengthen the courts and enhance their capacity to serve as agencies of societal harmony and stability capable of enforcing apolitical judgments in an otherwise divided polity.

Reestablishing the old form of judicial conservatism would also affect the judicial selection process. Judges would no longer be selected because of an expectation that they will pursue particular policies once they are on the bench. Instead, judges would be chosen for their intellectual acuity, their experience, and their professional attainments. In the world of today's judicial policymaking, it is inconceivable that a Herbert Hoover would appoint a Benjamin Cardozo to the Supreme Court, or a Dwight Eisenhower, a William Brennan. It accordingly might be necessary to return to the conservatism of a century ago to get intellectual giants rather than political operatives on the bench.

Returning to the old conservatism, however, would come at a huge cost. Most Americans today appear to feel that forces beyond their control are oppressing them and preventing them from achieving the good life they desire and believe Americans deserve. Although the American people disagree sharply about the identity of what is oppressing them, all are demanding an end to oppression. They are demanding the good life, and when legislatures fail to provide it, they turn to the judiciary for help. A judiciary modeled on the conservative judiciary of a century ago would not provide that help, and therefore neither activists on the left nor activists on the right would respect and support it.

Both the left and the right apparently prefer continuing to fight to gain control of the judiciary rather than fight to gain control of the legislature to attain the results they desire.

It is difficult finally to contemplate a revival of the old conservatism because of the manner in which that conservatism is connected to changing conceptions of justice. A prevalent conception today is that a person is being treated justly only if she can pursue her life's goals without obstruction by people or entities more powerful than herself. Concepts of equality are triumphant. Judicial conservatives in the decades after the Civil War understood, in contrast, that some people were entitled to more power than others and that those who possessed greater power behaved justly as long as they used their power within bounds permitted by precedent. It is difficult, indeed, to imagine such a hierarchical conception of justice becoming acceptable in the egalitarian America of today.

Notes

Introduction

1. Morton J. Horwitz, *The Transformation of American Law, 1870–1960: The Crisis of Legal Orthodoxy* (New York: Oxford University Press, 1992), 7.

2. Horwitz, *Transformation of American Law, 1870–1960*, 7.

3. Horwitz, *Transformation of American Law, 1870–1960*, 4.

4. Horwitz, *Transformation of American Law, 1870–1960*, 11.

5. Horwitz, *Transformation of American Law, 1870–1960*, 11 (emphasis added).

6. Horwitz, *Transformation of American Law, 1870–1960*, 119, 21–22.

7. Arnold M. Paul, *Conservative Crisis and the Rule of Law: Attitudes of the Bar and Bench, 1887–1895* (Ithaca, NY: Cornell University Press, 1960), 2.

8. Paul, *Conservative Crisis and the Rule of Law*, 221.

9. Paul, *Conservative Crisis and the Rule of Law*, 229–230, 235.

10. Charles Warren, *The Supreme Court in United States History*, 2 vols. (Boston: Little, Brown, rev. ed., 1926).

11. Warren, *The Supreme Court in United States History*, 702, 699–705.

12. Brian Z. Tamanaha, *Beyond the Formalist-Realist Divide: The Role of Politics in Judging* (Princeton, NJ: Princeton University Press, 2010), 6.

13. David M. Rabban, *Law's History: American Legal Thought and the Transatlantic Turn to History* (Cambridge: Cambridge University Press, 2013), 2.

14. *See generally* Rabban, *Law's History.*

15. *See* Roscoe Pound, "The Causes of Popular Dissatisfaction with the Administration of Justice," *American Law Review* 40 (1906): 729; Roscoe Pound, "Mechanical Jurisprudence," *Columbia Law Review* 8 (1908): 605.

16. *See* Robert Hale, "Coercion and Distribution in a Supposedly Non-Coercive State," *Political Science Quarterly* 38 (1923): 470.

17. *See* Felix Frankfurter and Nathan Greene, *The Labor Injunction* (New York: Macmillan, 1930).

18. Park & Sons Co. v. National Wholesale Druggists Assn, 175 N.Y. 1, 14 (1903).

19. *See* Brian Z. Tamanaha, "Understanding Legal Realism," 87 *Texas L. Rev.* 731, 782 (2009).

20. John Fabian Witt, *The Accidental Republic: Crippled Workingmen, Destitute Widows, and the Remaking of American Law* (Cambridge, MA: Harvard University Press, 2004), 159.

21. 60 U.S. 393 (1857).

22. Hepburn v. Griswold, 75 U.S. 603 (1870), and Legal Tender Cases, 79 U.S. 457 (1871).

23. *See* William E. Nelson, *The Roots of American Bureaucracy, 1830–1900* (Cambridge, MA: Harvard University Press, 1982), 59–61, 68–73.

24. "Current Topics," 1 *Albany L.J.* 270, 271 (1870).

25. *Quoted in* Charles Francis Adams Jr. and Henry Adams, *Chapters of Erie* (Ithaca, NY: Cornell University Press, 1956), 83. This book was originally published in 1886, and the article from which the quotation in the text is taken was first published in 1868.

26. Adams and Adams, *Chapters of Erie*, 86–87, 110, 159–160. *See generally id.* at 1–100, 137–193.

27. *See* Bruce A. Kimball, *The Inception of Modern Professional Education: C. C. Langdell, 1826–1906* (Chapel Hill: University of North Carolina Press, 2009), 6983.

28. "The Bar Association of New York," *Albany Law Journal* 1 (1870): 203.

29. *See* Nelson, *The Roots of American Bureaucracy*, 146–147.

30. *See generally* Nelson, *The Roots of American Bureaucracy*, 82–112, 140–148.

31. "Stare Decisis," *Albany Law Journal* 6 (1872): 329.

32. H. Campbell Black, "Principle of Stare Decisis," *American Law Register* 34 (1886): 745, 745–746, quoting Kent's *Commentaries on American Law.*

33. William Green, "Stare Decisis," *American Law Review* 14 (1880): 609, 639.

34. In the late nineteenth century, the general term of the Supreme Court had review jurisdiction over trial courts; since the end of that century, the appellate division of the Supreme Court has served as an intermediate appellate court between trial courts and the court of appeals.

35. Cross v. United States Trust Co. of New York, 131 N.Y. 330, 343–344 (1892).

36. 131 N.Y. at 344.

37. 131 N.Y. at 349.

38. 131 N.Y. at 344.

39. Lancaster v. Amsterdam Imp. Co., 140 N.Y. 576, 592 (1894).

40. People v. Hawkins, 157 N.Y. 1, 12 (1898).

41. Hubbard v. Hubbard, 228 N.Y. 81, 85 (1920).

42. Richardson v. Crandell, 48 N.Y. 348, 363 (1872). *Accord, e.g.*, Moss v. Cohen, 158 N.Y. 240, 248 (1899); Perkins v. Heert, 158 N.Y. 306, 312 (1899).

43. In re Lampson's Will, 161 N.Y. 511, 519 (1900).

44. 184 N.Y. 421 (1906).

45. Witt, *The Accidental Republic*, 159.

46. Rabban, *Law's History*, 27 (summarizing the thought of Thomas M. Cooley), 317 (summarizing the thought of James Bradley Thayer).

47. Speech by Abraham S. Hewitt in the House of Representatives, May 25, 1876, *quoted in* Nelson, *Roots of American Bureaucracy*, 87.

48. *See* Nelson, *Roots of American Bureaucracy*, 83–99.

49. "The Bar Association of New York," *Albany Law Journal* 1 (1870): 203. As the *New York Times* noted, judges were "compelled to pay . . . regard to [the] collective power" of the profession and thus followed the bar in its recourse to the past. "Editorial," *New York Times*, June 20, 1869, *quoted in* George W. Martin, *Causes and Conflicts: The Centennial History of the Association of the Bar of the City of New York, 1870–1970* (Boston: Houghton Mifflin, 1970), 12.

50. John Adams, *Diary and Autobiography*, ed. L. H. Butterfield, 1 (Cambridge, MA: Harvard University Press, 1961), 167.

51. Massachusetts Constitution, Part the First, art. *See* R. B. Bernstein, *The Education of John Adams* (New York: Oxford University Press, 2020), 4–5, 21, 22–38, 105–109, 237; Introduction, *in* Oscar Handlin and Mary F. Handlin, eds., *The Popular Sources of Political Authority: Documents on the Massachusetts Constitution of 1780* (Cambridge, MA: Harvard University Press, 1966), 1–54.

52. 5 U.S. (1 Cranch) 137 (1803).

53. *See* William E. Nelson, *Marbury v. Madison: The Origins and Legacy of Judicial Review*, 2nd ed. (Lawrence: University Press of Kansas, 2018), 94–106.

Chapter 1. Judicial Deference to Progressive Legislation

1. 198 U.S. 45 (1905). For a revisionist interpretation of the Supreme Court's *Lochner* decision, *see* David E. Bernstein, *Rehabilitating Lochner: Defending Individual Rights against Progressive Reform* (Chicago, IL: University of Chicago Press, 2011).

2. People v. Lochner, 177 N.Y. 145, 152 (1904).

3. 177 N.Y. at 150–151.

4. 177 N.Y. at 153.

5. 98 N.Y. 98 (1885).

6. 98 N.Y. at 113–114.

7. Park & Sons Co. v. National Wholesale Druggists Ass'n, 175 N.Y. 1, 14 (1903).

8. 201 N.Y. 271 (1911).

9. *See* N.Y. Constitution, art. 1, sec. 19 (1913) (art. 1, sec. 18 in present constitution).

10. *See* N.Y. Laws of 1914, ch. 41.

11. 215 N.Y. 514 (1915), *revd on other grounds*, Southern Pacific Co. v. Jensen, 244 U.S. 205 (1917). *Accord*, Clyde Steamship Co. v. Walker, 244 U.S. 255 (1917), *revg*, Walker v. Clyde Steamship Co., 215 N.Y. 529 (1915).

12. People v. Windholz, 86 N.Y. Supp. 1015, 1017 (4th Dept. 1904) (dictum).

13. *See* People v. Marx, 99 N.Y. 377 (1885).

14. *See* People v. Warren, 34 N.Y. Supp. 942 (Super. Ct. Buffalo 1895). The *Warren* case was overruled twenty years later by People v. Crane, 214 N.Y. 154, *aff'd*, Crane v. New York, 239 U.S. 195 (1915), which upheld legislation prohibiting employment of aliens on public works.

15. *See* People v. Biesecker, 68 N.Y. Supp. 1067 (1st Dept.), *aff'd*, 169 N.Y. 53 (1901).

16. *See* New York Sanitary Utilization Co. v. Dept of Health of City of New York, 70 N.Y. Supp. 510 (1st Dept. 1901). For an earlier case acquitting a defendant charged with violating similar legislation, *see* People v. Rosenberg, 138 N.Y. 410 (1893).

17. *See* People v. Beattie, 89 N.Y. Supp. 193 (1st Dept. 1904).

18. *See* People ex rel. Duryea v. Wilber, 198 N.Y. 1 (1910).

19. *See* People v. Ringe, 197 N.Y. 143 (1910).

20. *See* Hauser v. North British and Mercantile Ins. Co., 206 N.Y. 455 (1912).

21. *See* People v. Horwitz, 140 N.Y. Supp. 437 (N.Y. City Magistrates Ct. 1912). *Cf.* People v. Green, 83 N.Y. Supp. 460 (1st Dept. 1903) (prohibiting advertisements on land facing parks); City of Watertown v. Rodenbaugh, 98 N.Y. Supp. 885 (4th Dept. 1906) (prohibiting bill posting, bill distributing, or distributing samples); People ex rel. M. Wineburgh Advertising Co., 113 N.Y. Supp. 855 (1st Dept. 1908), *aff'd*, 195 N.Y. 126 (1909) (prohibiting signs larger than of a specified size); Hellinger v. City of New York, 168 N.Y. Supp. 271 (1st Dept. 1917) (unlawful for city to build ornamental structure that obstructs adjoining owners light); People ex rel. Standard Bill Posting Co. v. Hastings, 137 N.Y. Supp. 186 (Sup. Ct. Orange Co.), *aff'd*, 138 N.Y. Supp. 1138 (2d Dept. 1912), *aff'd*, 207 N.Y. 763 (1913) (requiring that billboards be constructed of metal).

22. *See* People ex rel. Treat v. Coler, 166 N.Y. 144 (1901).

23. *See* People v. Beakes Dairy Co., 166 N.Y. Supp. 209 (3d Dept. 1917), *aff'd*, 222 N.Y. 416 (1918).

24. *See* People ex rel. Tyroler v. City Prison of City of New York, 157 N.Y. 116 (1898); People ex rel. Fleischmann v. Caldwell, 71 N.Y. Supp. 654 (4th Dept.), *aff'd*, 168 N.Y. 671 (1901); People ex rel. Appel v. Zimmerman, 92 N.Y. Supp. 497 (4th Dept. 1905); People ex rel. Weil v. Hagan, 71 N.Y. Supp. 461 (Sup. Ct. N.Y. Co. 1901).

25. *See* White, Corbin & Co. v. Jones, 167 N.Y. 158 (1901); Bronk v. Barckley, 43 N.Y. Supp. 400 (3d Dept. 1897).

26. *See* Fox v. Mohawk and Hudson River Humane Socy, 165 N.Y. 517 (1901).

27. *See* People ex rel. Shand v. Tighe, 30 N.Y. Supp. 368 (1894).

28. *See* City of Brooklyn v. Franz, 33 N.Y. Supp. 869 (2d Dept. 1895).

29. *See* Webb v. Mayor of City of New York, 64 How. Pr. 10 (Sup. Ct. N.Y. Co. 1882).

30. *See* People ex rel. Dilzer v. Calder, 85 N.Y. Supp. 1015 (2d Dept. 1903). *Cf.* Morton v. Mayor of City of New York, 140 N.Y. 207 (1893) (prohibiting location of pumping station adjacent to adjoining property).

31. *See* People ex rel. McPike v. Van De Carr, 178 N.Y. 425 (1904).

32. *See* Lee v. OMalley, 125 N.Y. Supp. 772 (1st Dept. 1910), *revg*, Lee v. OMalley, 126 N.Y. Supp. 775 (Sup. Ct. N.Y. Co. 1910).

33. *See* People ex rel. Goff v. Kirk, 119 N.Y. Supp. 862 (3d Dept. 1909).

34. *See* Frank L. Fisher Co. v. Woods, 187 N.Y. 90 (1907).

35. *See* People v. Gillson, 109 N.Y. 389 (1888)

36. *See* Wright v. Hart, 182 N.Y. 330 (1905).

37. *See* Warsaw Water Works Co. v. Village of Warsaw, 161 N.Y. 176 (1899). *Cf.* Village of Saratoga Springs v. Saratoga Gas, Elec. Light & Power Co., 191 N.Y. 123 (1908) (statute struck down for failure to allow company to apply for rate increase after specified period of time).

38. *See* Beardsley v. New York, Lake Erie & W.R.R. Co., 162 N.Y. 230 (1900); Rochester & C. Turnpike-Road Co. v. Joel, 58 N.Y. Supp. 346 (4th Dept. 1899); Wilson v. United Traction Co., 76 N.Y. Supp. 203 (3d Dept. 1902).

39. *See* Mayor of City of New York v. Manhattan Ry. Co., 143 N.Y. 1 (1894); Lehigh Valley Ry. Co. v. Adam, 176 N.Y. 420 (1903); City of Binghamton v. Binghamton & P.D. Ry. Co., 16 N.Y. Supp. 225 (4th Dept. 1891). *Cf.* Reining v. New York, Lackawanna & Western Ry. Co., 128 N.Y. 157 (1891) (substantial closure of street constitutes taking of abutting property); Stroub v. Manhattan Ry. Co., 15 N.Y. Supp. 135 (1st Dept. 1891) (additional track placing added burden on plaintiffs property constitutes a taking).

40. *See* People v. OBrien, 111 N.Y. 1 (1888). For additional miscellaneous cases holding legislation unconstitutional, *see* People ex rel. Manhattan Sav. Inst. v. Otis, 90 N.Y. 48 (1882); Matter of Tuthill, 163 N.Y. 133 (1900); Boswell v. Security Mutual Life Ins. Co., 193 N.Y. 465 (1908); In re Cook, 83 N.Y. Supp. 1009 (3d Dept. 1903); Haefelein v. Jacob, 94 N.Y. Supp. 466 (2d Dept. 1905); City of New York v. New York City Ry. Co., 117 N.Y. Supp. 921 (App. Term 1909), *aff'd*, 203 N.Y. 593 (1911); Johnstown Cemetery Assn v. Parker, 59 N.Y. Supp. 821 (Sup. Ct. Fulton Co.), *aff'd*, 60 N.Y. Supp. 1015 (3d Dept. 1899); People v. McFall, 158 N.Y. Supp. 974 (Buffalo City Ct. 1916).

41. People ex rel. Armstrong v. Warden of City Prison of City of New York, 183 N.Y. 223, 226 (1905) (emphasis added).

42. People v. Goldberger, 163 N.Y. Supp. 663, 666 (N.Y. City Ct. Special Sess. 1916).

43. 27 N.Y. 400 (1863).

44. 27 N.Y. at 415.

45. 27 N.Y. at 405.

46. 27 N.Y. at 429.

47. 31 N.Y. 164 (1865). *See also* Robinson v. Intl Life Assurance Socy of

London, 42 N.Y. 54 (1870) (payment in June 1861 in Confederate dollars of premium due on life insurance policy sufficient to keep policy in force).

48. *See* N.Y. Laws of 1855, ch. 428.

49. *See* Reynolds v. Schultz, 27 N.Y. Super. Ct. 282 (Super. Ct. N.Y. Co. 1867). *Accord,* Coe v. Schultz, 47 Barb. 64 (Sup. Ct. N.Y. Co. 1866).

50. *See* Metropolitan Board of Health v. Heister, 37 N.Y. 661 (1868).

51. *See* Roosevelt v. Godard, 52 Barb. 533 (Gen. Term N.Y. Co. 1868).

52. *See* Campbell v. Evans, 45 N.Y. 356 (1871).

53. *See* Phelps v. Racey, 60 N.Y. 10 (1875). *Accord,* People v. Clair, 221 N.Y. 108 (1917); People v. Cohen, 86 N.Y. Supp. 475 (1st Dept. 1904); People v. Waldorf-Astoria Hotel Co., 103 N.Y. Supp. 434 (1st Dept. 1907). *Cf.* Lawton v. Steele, 119 N.Y. 226 (1890), *aff'd,* 152 U.S. 133 (1894) (prohibition on taking fish with nets in specified waters); People v. Lowndes, 130 N.Y. 455 (1892) (prohibition on nonresidents gathering oysters in state waters); Barrett v. State of New York, 220 N.Y. 423 (1917) (state not liable for damages caused by wild beaver protected from death by conservation laws).

54. *See* Polinsky v. People, 73 N.Y. 65 (1878). Regulation of the dairy industry continued throughout the six decades under study herein. *See, e.g.,* Monroe Dairy Ass'n v. Stanley, 20 N.Y. Supp. 19 (2d Dept. 1892); People ex rel. Schulz v. Hamilton, 177 N.Y. Supp. 222 (4th Dept. 1919). *See also* People ex rel. Lodes v. Department of Health of City of New York, 189 N.Y. 187 (1907) (discussing procedure for challenging administrative revocation of license in court).

55. *See* Bertholf v. OReilly, 74 N.Y. 509 (1878). *See also* People ex rel. Doscher v. Sisson, 222 N.Y. 387 (1918) (upholding legislation prohibiting sale of liquor near military camps and factories manufacturing munitions during World War I).

56. *See* People v. Globe Mutual Life Ins. Co., 60 How. Pr. 82 (Sup. Ct. Albany Co. 1880). *Accord,* Lord v. Equitable Life Assurance Socy, 194 N.Y. 212 (1909). For regulation of out-of-state companies, *see* People v. Formosa, 131 N.Y. 478 (1892).

57. 99 N.Y. 377 (1885).

58. *See* People v. Arensberg, 105 N.Y. 123 (1887). *Accord,* People v. Girard, 145 N.Y. 105 (1895) (prohibition on addition of artificial color to vinegar).

59. *See* People ex rel. New York Elec. Lines Co. v. Squire, 107 N.Y. 593 (1888), *aff'd,* 145 U.S. 175 (1892).

60. People v. King, 110 N.Y. 418, 419, 426 (1888).

61. *See* American Rapid Telegraph Co. v. Hess, 125 N.Y. 641 (1891). *Cf.*

City of Philadelphia v. Postal Telegraph Cable Co., 21 N.Y. Supp. 556 (1st Dept. 1892) (upholding license fees on telegraph poles and wires).

62. *See* People ex rel. Oak Hill Cemetery Assn v. Pratt, 129 N.Y. 68 (1891). *Cf.* City of New York v. Kelsey, 213 N.Y. 638 (1914), *aff'g*, 143 N.Y. Supp. 21 (2d Dept. 1913) (enjoining location of cemetery within one-half mile of city reservoir); Gordon v. Village of Silver Creek, 112 N.Y. Supp. 54 (4th Dept. 1908), *aff'd*, 197 N.Y. 509 (1909) (granting damages for smoke pollution from coal-fired pumping station).

63. *See* In re Long Island R.R. Co., 21 N.Y. Supp. 489 (2d Dept. 1892).

64. People ex rel. Nechamcus v. Warden of the City Prison, 144 N.Y. 529, 536 (1895).

65. *See* Ford v. New York Central R.R. Co., 53 N.Y. Supp. 764 (4th Dept. 1898)

66. 145 N.Y. 32 (1895).

67. N.Y. Laws of 1887, ch. 84, sec. 11.

68. 145 N.Y. at 42.

69. Tenement House Dept of City of New York v. Moeschen, 179 N.Y. 325 (1904), *aff'd*, 203 U.S. 583 (1906).

70. N.Y. Laws of 1901, ch. 334, sec. 100.

71. 179 N.Y. at 332–333. The 1901 act was applied retroactively to buildings under construction when the act took effect. *See* City of New York v. Herdje, 74 N.Y. Supp. 104 (2d Dept. 1902).

72. *See* Cockcroft v. Mitchell, 167 N.Y. Supp. 6 (Sup. Ct. N.Y. Co. 1917).

73. *See* People v. Kaye, 212 N.Y. 407 (1914). *See also* Waldo v. Christman, 130 N.Y. Supp. 260 (App. Term 1911) (requiring owners of specified sorts of buildings to provide fire alarms and fire extinguishers).

74. *See* City of New York v. Foster, 205 N.Y. 593 (1912), *aff'g*, 133 N.Y. Supp. 152 (1st Dept. 1911).

75. 215 N.Y. 514 (1915), *rev'd on other grounds*, Southern Pacific Co. v. Jensen, 244 U.S. 204 (1917).

76. 229 N.Y. 313 (1920). *Cf.* In re Russell, 158 N.Y. Supp. 162 (Sup. Ct. Niagara Co. 1916) (upholding city ordinance prohibiting factories in specified part of city).

77. *See* Bandel v. City of New York, 204 N.Y. 683 (1912).

78. *See* City of Buffalo v. Hill, 79 N.Y. Supp. 449 (4th Dept. 1903).

79. *See* Viemeister v. White, 179 N.Y. 235 (1904). *Cf.* People v. Pierson, 176 N.Y. 201 (1903) (upholding indictment of parent who failed to obtain doctor for sick child who subsequently died).

80. *See* People ex rel. Armstrong v. Warden of City Prison of City of New York, 183 N.Y. 223 (1905).

81. *See* Hathorn v. Natural Carbonic Gas Co., 194 N.Y. 326 (1909). *But see* People v. New York Carbonic Gas Co., 196 N.Y. 421 (1909) (narrowing the holding of the *Hathorn* case).

82. *See* People v. Luhrs, 195 N.Y. 377 (1909).

83. *See* Musco v. United Surety Co., 196 N.Y. 459 (1909).

84. *See* Bush v. New York Life Ins. Co., 119 N.Y. Supp. 796 (1st Dept. 1909); Stern v. Metropolitan Life Ins. Co., 154 N.Y. Supp. 472 (1st Dept. 1915), *aff'd*, 217 N.Y. 626 (1916).

85. *See* McIntosh v. Johnson, 211 N.Y. 265 (1914); Stubbe v. Adamson, 220 N.Y. 459 (1917).

86. *See* Matter of New York Protestant Episcopal Public School, 46 N.Y. 178 (1871).

87. *See* City of Rochester v. Gutberlett, 211 N.Y. 309 (1914).

88. *See* People v. Griswold, 213 N.Y. 92 (1914). *See also* Matter of Lewis, 178 N.Y. Supp. 533 (3d Dept. 1919) (prohibiting practice of dentistry by corporations). *Cf.* Co-Operative Law Co. v. McDermott, 198 N.Y. 479 (1910) (prohibiting practice of law by corporations); People ex rel. Trojan Realty Co. v. Purdy, 162 N.Y. Supp. 56 (1st Dept. 1916) (noting in dictum that corporations also could not practice law).

89. *See* Hirshfeld v. Bopp, 145 N.Y. 84 (1895); Greenspan v. Oliner, 149 N.Y. Supp. 752 (3d Dept. 1914); Richards v. Schwab, 167 N.Y. Supp. 535 (Sup. Ct. N.Y. Co. 1917); Persons v. Gardner, 56 N.Y. Supp. 822 (Sup. Ct. Erie Co.), *aff'd*, 59 N.Y. Supp. 463 (4th Dept. 1899).

90. *See* People ex rel. Van Norder v. Sewer, Water, and Street Commn of Village of Saratoga Springs, 86 N.Y. Supp. 445 (3d Dept. 1904). *Cf.* Hilliard Hotel Co. v. City of New York, 211 N.Y. 597 (1914) (location of hack stand outside hotel without permission of hotel).

91. *See* People v. Roemer, 153 N.Y. Supp. 323 (2d Dept. 1915).

92. *See* People v. Bishopp, 89 N.Y. Supp. 709 (Sup. Ct. Madison Co. 1904), *aff'd*, 94 N.Y. Supp. 773 (3d Dept. 1905). *Cf.* Williams v. Rivenburg, 129 N.Y. Supp. 473 (4th Dept. 1911) (prohibiting sale of calves less than four weeks old).

93. *See* People v. Goldberger, 163 N.Y. Supp. 663 (Ct. Special Sess. N.Y. City 1916).

94. *See* Bronx Gas & Elec. Co. v. Public Service Commn, 180 N.Y. Supp. 38, 43 (1st Dept. 1919).

95. *See* Richman v. Consolidated Gas Co. of New York, 100 N.Y. Supp. 81, 85 (1st Dept.), *aff'd*, 186 N.Y. 209 (1906). *See also* Matter of Rebecchi, 100 N.Y. Supp. 335 (Sup. Ct. N.Y. Co. 1906) (rates must be based on current value of property, not original capitalization).

96. *See* Buffalo East Side R.R. Co. v. Buffalo Street R.R. Co., 111 N.Y. 132 (1888); People v. Budd, 117 N.Y. 1 (1889), *aff'd*, Budd v. New York, 143 U.S. 517 (1892); Brooklyn Union Gas Co. v. City of New York, 188 N.Y. 334 (1907); Willis v. City of Rochester, 219 N.Y. 427 (1916).

97. *See* People ex rel. Central Park, North and East River R.R. Co. v. Willcox, 194 N.Y. 383 (1909); People ex rel. Cohoes Ry. Co. v. Public Service Commn, 202 N.Y. 547 (1911); People ex rel. Village of South Glens Falls v. Public Service Commn, 225 N.Y. 216 (1919).

98. *See* New York & Oswego Midland R.R. Co. v. Van Horn, 57 N.Y. 473 (1874).

99. *See* Matter of New York Cable Co. v. Mayor of City of New York, 104 N.Y. 1 (1886).

100. *See* Parfitt v. Furguson, 38 N.Y. Supp. 466 (2d Dept. 1896). *See also* Attorney General v. Consol. Gas Co. of New York, 108 N.Y. Supp. 823 (1st Dept. 1908) (upholding right of merged gas company to lay mains in city street).

101. *See* City of Buffalo v. Buffalo Gas Co., 80 N.Y. Supp. 1093 (4th Dept. 1903).

102. *See* People v. Long Island R.R. Co., 134 N.Y. 506 (1892).

103. *See* People v. Delaware & Hudson Canal Co., 52 N.Y. Supp. 850 (3d Dept. 1898), *aff'd*, 165 N.Y. 362 (1901).

104. *See* Binninger v. City of New York, 177 N.Y. 199 (1904); People v. New York Central R.R. Co., 206 N.Y. 274 (1912); People ex rel. Lucey v. Molloy, 54 N.Y. Supp. 1084 (3d Dept. 1898), *aff'd*, 161 N.Y. 621 (1899); Weed v. City of Binghamton, 71 N.Y. Supp. 282 (3d Dept. 1901). *Cf.* City of Buffalo v. Delaware, Lackawanna & Western R.R. Co., 204 N.Y. 562 (1912), *affg*, 120 N.Y. Supp. 1081 (4th Dept. 1910) (city may direct railroad to build moveable rather than fixed bridge over river).

105. *See* Matter of New York Elevated R.R. Co., 70 N.Y. 327 (1877); Matter of Gilbert Elevated Ry. Co. v. Kobbe, 70 N.Y. 361 (1877); Matter of Thirty-Fourth St. R.R. Co., 102 N.Y. 343 (1886); New York Cable Co. v. Mayor of City of New York, 104 N.Y. 1 (1886). *Cf.* Fort Plain Bridge Co. v. Smith, 30 N.Y. 44 (1864) (legislature may construct second bridge adjacent to preexisting private bridge); Matter of Sackett, Douglas & DeGraw Streets, 74 N.Y. 95 (1878) (legislature determines when and

where streets are to be constructed); Matter of City of New York, 68 N.Y. Supp. 196 (2d Dept.), *aff'd*, 167 N.Y. 624 (1901) (legislature determines when and where streets are to be constructed); Skaneateles Water Works Co. v. Village of Skaneateles, 161 N.Y. 154 (1899), *aff'd*, 184 U.S.[54] (1902) (municipality may enter into competition with private water company); Sixth Avenue R.R. Co. v. Gilbert Elevated Ry. Co., 43 N.Y. Super. Ct. 292 (Super. Ct. N.Y. Co. 1878) (legislature may authorize building of new railroad on same route as existing railroad); People ex rel. Weed-Parsons Printing Co. v. Palmer, 41 N.Y. Supp. 878 (Sup. Ct. Albany Co. 1896) (legislature may authorize state official to make contract in breach of preexisting contract).

106. *See* People ex rel. Schurz v. Cook, 110 N.Y. 443 (1888), *aff'd*, 148 U.S. 397 (1893); People v. Ulster & Delaware R.R. Co., 128 N.Y. 240 (1891); People ex rel. Westchester St. R.R. Co. v. Public Service Commn, 143 N.Y. Supp. 148 (3d Dept. 1913), *modified*, 210 N.Y. 456 (1914); City of Rochester v. Bronson, 41 How. Pr. 78 (4th Dept. 1871). *Cf.* Lord v. Thomas, 64 N.Y. 107 (1876) (state may cease work on public project); People v. Brooklyn, Flatbush & Coney Island Ry. Co., 89 N.Y. 75 (1882) (allowing railroad to use steam power on Atlantic Avenue); People ex rel. Mitchell v. Lawrence, 54 Barb. 589 (Gen. Term Warren Co. 1869) (upholding statute declaring abandoned plank roads to be public highways).

107. Rhodes v. Sperry & Hutchinson Co., 193 N.Y. 223, 228 (1908), *aff'd*, Sperry & Hutchinson Co. V. Rhodes, 220 U.S. 502 (1911). *Accord*, Binns v. Vitagraph Company of America, 210 N.Y. 51 (1913).

108. *See* Matter of Davies, 168 N.Y. 89 (1901).

109. *See* Cleveland v. City of Watertown, 222 N.Y. 159 (1917).

110. *See* People ex rel. Devery v. Coler, 173 N.Y. 103 (1903).

111. *See* People ex rel. Welch v. Bard, 209 N.Y. 304 (1913).

112. *See* Buckbee v. Board of Educ. of City of New York, 100 N.Y. Supp. 943 (1st Dept. 1906), *aff'd*, 187 N.Y. 544 (1907).

113. *See* MacMullen v. City of Middletown, 187 N.Y. 37 (1907).

114. *See* Brearley School v. Ward, 201 N.Y. 358 (1911); Stiefel v. New York Novelty Co., 55 N.Y. Supp. 90 (Sup. Ct. N.Y. Co. 1898).

115. *See* U.S. Constitution amend. 5; N.Y. Constitution, art. 1, sec. 7.

116. *See* Matter of New York & Harlem R.R. Co. v. Kip, 46 N.Y. 546 (1871); Matter of New York Central R.R. Co v. Metropolitan Gas-Light Co., 63 N.Y. 326 (1875). *Cf.* Peoples Rapid Transit Co. v. Dash, 125 N.Y. 93 (1890) (railroads may build only under authority of and subject to regulations of government).

117. *See* Matter of Pierce, 172 N.Y. Supp. 852 (4th Dept. 1918).

118. *See* Oneonta Light & Power Co. v. Schwarzenbach, 150 N.Y. Supp. 76 (3d Dept. 1914), *aff'd*, 219 N.Y. 588 (1916).

119. *See* Matter of Bloomfield & Rochester Natural Gas Co., 63 Barb. 437 (4th Dept. 1872).

120. *See* Richards v. Citizens Water Supply Co., 125 N.Y. Supp. 116 (2d Dept. 1910).

121. *See* Matter of Lyons Cemetery Ass'n, 86 N.Y. Supp. 960 (4th Dept. 1904). But a cemetery that did not allow for the burial of all people equally could not exercise eminent domain power. *See* Matter of Deansville Cemetery Ass'n, 66 N.Y. 569 (1876); Stannards Corners Rural Cemetery Ass'n v. Brandes, 35 N.Y. Supp. 674 (Sup. Ct. Allegany Co. 1895).

122. *See* Bunyan v. Commrs of Palisades Interstate Park, 153 N.Y. Supp. 622 (3d Dept. 1915).

123. *See* Matter of Central Park Extension, 16 Abb. Pr. 56 (Sup. Ct. N.Y. Co. 1863). *Accord*, Matter of City of Rochester, 137 N.Y. 243 (1893).

124. *See* Matter of Town of Whitestown, 53 N.Y. Supp. 397 (County Ct. Oneida Co. 1898).

125. *See* Matter of Tuthill, 50 N.Y. Supp. 410 (County Ct. Orange Co. 1898), *revd*, 55 N.Y. Supp. 657 (2d Dept. 1899), *aff'd*, 163 N.Y. 133 (1900); People ex rel. Pulman v. Henion, 19 N.Y. Supp. 488 (5th Dept. 1892).

126. *See* N.Y. Laws of 1915, ch. 717.

127. *See* Flood Abatement Commn of Olean v. Merritt, 158 N.Y. Supp. 289 (Sup. Ct. Cattaraugus Co. 1916).

128. *See* Rensselaer & Saratoga R.R. Co. v. Davis, 43 N.Y. 137 (1870); Mairs v. Manhattan Real Estate Ass'n, 89 N.Y. 498 (1882); Queens Terminal Co. v. Schmuck, 132 N.Y. Supp. 159 (2d Dept. 1911). Thus, land that had been condemned for a railroad yard could not subsequently be condemned for a street. *See* Matter of City of New York, 226 N.Y. 128 (1919).

129. *See* Ashby v. State, 175 N.Y. Supp. 312 (Ct. Claims 1918). *Cf.* Remington v. State, 101 N.Y. Supp. 952 (3d Dept. 1906) (state's entry upon land with consent of supposed but not actual owner a trespass).

130. *See* Struve v. Droge, 62 How. Pr. 233 (Ct. Com. Pleas N.Y. Co. 1881). But, in dictum, the court stated that if a fire had actually existed, there would be no trespass and no damages.

131. *See* Mahady v. Bushwick R.R. Co., 91 N.Y. 148 (1883) (dictum); Lahr v. Metropolitan Elevated Ry. Co., 104 N.Y. 268 (1887); Abendroth v. Manhattan Ry. Co., 122 N.Y. 1 (1890); Kane v. New York Elevated R.R. Co., 125 N.Y. 164 (1891); Sperb v. Metropolitan Elevated Ry. Co., 137 N.Y.

155 (1893); Knoth v. Manhattan Ry. Co., 187 N.Y. 243 (1907); Matter of Mayor of City of New York, 197 N.Y. 518 (1909); Bradley v. Degnon Contracting Co., 224 N.Y. 60 (1918). Owners of land that did not abut on obstructed streets had no remedy for the obstruction; *see* Matter of Grade Crossing Commrs of City of Buffalo, 207 N.Y. 52 (1912). Nor did owners of abutting land when an obstruction was created by a private entity in pursuit of statutory requirements. *See* Fries v. New York & Harlem R.R. Co., 169 N.Y. 270 (1901). *But see* Lewis v. New York & Harlem R.R. Co., 162 N.Y. 202 (1900).

132. *See* Roddy v. Brooklyn City & Newton R.R. Co., 52 N.Y. Supp. 1025 (2d Dept. 1898).

133. *See* Huffmire v. City of Brooklyn, 162 N.Y. 584 (1900). *But cf.* First Construction Co. of Brooklyn v. State, 221 N.Y. 295 (1917) (filled-in tidewater not property in absence of proper grant).

134. *See* Van Etten v. City of New York, 226 N.Y. 483 (1919). *But cf.* Champlain Stone & Sand Co. v. State, 127 N.Y. Supp. 131 (3d Dept. 1911), *aff'd*, 205 N.Y. 539 (1912) (bridge over stream widened to improve navigability not property for which compensation was required).

135. *See* People ex rel. Burhans v. City of New York, 198 N.Y. 439 (1910); Brooklyn Trust Co. v. City of New York, 179 N.Y. Supp. 441 (Sup. Ct. Kings Co. 1919), *aff'd*, 190 N.Y. Supp. 812 (2d Dept. 1921), *aff'd*, 234 N.Y. 520 (1922). *But cf.* Matter of Board of Water Supply of City of New York, 142 N.Y. Supp. 801 (3d Dept.). *aff'd*, 209 N.Y. 572 (1913) (attorney's fees not allowable as costs in eminent domain proceeding).

136. *See* Watson v. New York Central R.R. Co., 47 N.Y. 157 (1872).

137. *See* Stevens v. New York Elevated R.R. Co., 130 N.Y. 95 (1891); Bischoff v. New York Elevated R.R. Co., 138 N.Y. 257 (1893); New York Mun. R.R. Corp. v. Weber, 226 N.Y. 70 (1919). They also upheld awards unsatisfactory to condemnees. *See* Matter of City of Brooklyn, 143 N.Y. 596 (1894), *aff'd*, Long Island Water-Supply Co. v. City of Brooklyn, 166 U.S. 685 (1897).

138. *See* People ex rel. Central Trust Co. v. Prendergast, 202 N.Y. 188 (1911).

139. *See* Slingerland v. Intl Contracting Co., 169 N.Y. 60 (1901). *Accord*, Fearing v. Irwin, 55 N.Y. 486 (1874); Matter of City of New York, 144 N.Y. Supp. 1002 (1st Dept. 1913), *aff'd*, 212 N.Y. 547 (1914).

140. *See* People ex rel. Crowell v. Lawrence, 36 Barb. 177 (Gen. Term Kings Co. 1862), *aff'd*, 41 N.Y. 137 (1869); Litchfield v. McComber, 42 Barb. 288 (Gen. Term Dutchess Co. 1864).

141. *See* Genet v. City of Brooklyn, 99 N.Y. 296 (1885).

142. Woodruff v. Oswego Starch Factory, 177 N.Y. 23, 28 (1903) (dictum).

143. *See* Gautier v. Ditmar, 204 N.Y. 20, 26 (1912) (dictum).

144. *See* People v. Fire Ass'n of Philadelphia, 92 N.Y. 311 (1883), *aff'd*, Philadelphia Fire Ass'n v. New York, 119 U.S. 110 (1886); Trustees of Exempt Firemen's Benevolent Fund of City of New York v. Roome, 93 N.Y. 313 (1883); Fire Dept of City of New York v. Stanton, 159 N.Y. 225 (1899).

145. *See* People ex rel. Hatch v. Reardon, 184 N.Y. 431 (1906), *aff'd*, 204 U.S. 152 (1907). *But cf.* People ex rel. Ferguson v. Reardon, 197 N.Y. 236 (1910) (provision for inspection of private books and papers of stockbrokers unconstitutional on grounds of self-incrimination).

146. *See* People ex rel. Eisman v. Ronner, 95 N.Y. Supp. 518 (Sup. Ct. N.Y. Co. 1905), *aff'd*, 97 N.Y. Supp. 550 (1st Dept.), *aff'd*, 185 N.Y. 285 (1906).

147. *See* Matter of Keeney, 194 N.Y. 281 (1909), *aff'd*, Keeney v. Comptroller of State of New York, 222 U.S. 525 (1912).

148. *See* People ex rel. Vandervoort Realty Co. v. Glynn, 194 N.Y. 387 (1909). *Accord*, In re Tiffany & Co., 30 N.Y. Supp. 494 (3d Dept. 1894) (franchise tax on manufacturing company); People ex rel. Bank for Sav. v. Miller, 82 N.Y. Supp. 621 (3d Dept. 1903), *modified*, 177 N.Y. 461 (1904) (franchise tax on bank).

149. *See* Eno v. Mayor of City of New York, 68 N.Y. 214 (1877) (dictum).

150. People ex rel. New York, O. & W. Ry. Co., 128 N.Y. Supp. 177, 180 (3d Dept.), *aff'd*, 202 N.Y. 556 (1911). *Accord*, People ex rel. Sheldon v. Fraser, 26 N.Y. Supp. 814 (3d Dept. 1893); People ex rel. Rochester Telephone Co. v. State Bd. of Tax Commrs, 134 N.Y. Supp. 987 (Sup. Ct. Monroe Co. 1912). *See also* People ex rel. Pells v. Bd. of Supervisors of Ulster County, 65 N.Y. 300 (1875) (court order to correct unequal assessment mandatory).

151. *See* People ex rel. Roosevelt Hospital v. Raymond, 194 N.Y. 189 (1909).

152. *See* Matter of Rochester Trust & Safe Deposit Co., 87 N.Y. Supp. 628 (Sup. Ct. Monroe Co. 1904).

153. *See* Dutchess County Mut. Ins. Co. v. City of Poughkeepsie, 4 N.Y. Supp. 93 (2d Dept. 1889).

154. *See* People ex rel. New York Central R.R. Co. v. Woodbury, 133 N.Y. Supp. 135 (Sup. Ct. Albany Co. 1910).

155. *See* People ex rel. Farrington v. Mensching, 187 N.Y. 8 (1907).

156. *See* Matter of Pell, 171 N.Y. 48 (1902).

Chapter 2. Labor Law

1. Kissam v. United States Printing Co., 199 N.Y. 76, 78 (1910).

2. 17 N.Y. Supp. 264 (Sup. Ct. Broome Co. 1891).

3. 17 N.Y. Supp. at 268–269.

4. Jacobs v. Cohen, 183 N.Y. 207, 210–211 (1905). *Accord*, Kissam v. United States Printing Co., 199 N.Y. 76 (1910). *But see* Curran v. Galen, 152 N.Y. 33 (1897) (declaring unlawful a contract between a union and a manufacturers association requiring all workers in the industry to become union members).

5. *See* Bossert v. Dhuy, 221 N.Y. 342 (1917).

6. Natl Protective Ass'n v. Cumming, 170 N.Y. 315, 320–321 (1902).

7. *See* People v. Marcus, 185 N.Y. 257 (1906).

8. 185 N.Y. at 264.

9. National Labor Relations Act, 49 Stat. 449 (1935).

10. *See* Davis v. United Portable Hoisting Engineers, 51 N.Y. Supp. 180, 182 (1st Dept. 1898). *Cf.* People v. Epstean, 170 N.Y. Supp. 68 (Gen. Sess. N.Y. Co. 1918) (upholding agreement between union and employers board of trade that union members will work only for members of board).

11. *See* Searle Mfg. Co. v. Terry, 106 N.Y. Supp. 438 (Sup. Ct. Ulster Co. 1905).

12. *See* City Trust, Safe Deposit & Surety Co. of Philadelphia v. Waldhauer, 95 N.Y. Supp. 222 (Sup. Ct. N.Y. Co. 1905).

13. Auburn Draying Co. v. Wardell, 227 N.Y. 1, 10 (1919).

14. Matter of McCormick, 117 N.Y. Supp. 70, 72–73 (1st Dept.), *aff'd*, 196 N.Y. 571 (1909).

15. Jones v. Maher, 116 N.Y. Supp. 180, 183 (Sup. Ct. Westchester Co. 1909), *aff'd*, 125 N.Y. Supp. 1126 (2d Dept. 1910).

16. Justin Seubert, Inc. v. Reiff, 164 N.Y. Supp. 522, 526 (Sup. Ct. Onondaga Co. 1917).

17. Bossert v. United Brotherhood of Carpenters & Joiners of America, 137 N.Y. Supp. 321, 323 (Sup. Ct. Kings Co. 1912).

18. 164 N.Y. Supp. 533 (Sup. Ct. Kings Co. 1917).

19. 164 N.Y. Supp. at 534–535.

20. 183 N.Y. Supp. 195 (Sup. Ct. Monroe Co. 1920).

21. 183 N.Y. Supp. at 200–201.

22. *See* Garside v. Hollywood, 150 N.Y. Supp. 647 (Sup. Ct. Kings Co. 1914); Grand Shoe Co. v. Children's Shoe Workers' Union, 187 N.Y. Supp. 886 (Sup. Ct. Kings Co. 1920).

23. *See* Welinsky v. Hillman, 185 N.Y. Supp. 257 (Sup. Ct. N.Y. Co. 1920).

24. *See* Grassi Contracting Co. v. Bennett, 160 N.Y. Supp. 279 (1st Dept. 1916).

25. *See* Rosenwasser Bros., Inc. v. Pepper, 172 N.Y. Supp. 310 (Sup. Ct. Queens Co. 1918).

26. 158 N.Y. 306 (1899).

27. 158 N.Y. at 311–312.

28. 158 N.Y. at 311.

29. 158 N.Y. at 312–313.

30. *See* New York Central R.R. Co. v. Williams, 199 N.Y. 108 (1910), *aff'd*, Erie R.R. Co. V, Williams, 233 U.S. 685 (1914).

31. 142 N.Y. 101 (1894).

32. 166 N.Y. 1 (1901).

33. 166 N.Y. at 21.

34. 166 N.Y. at 21.

35. *See also* Ewen v. Thompson-Starrett Co., 208 N.Y. 245 (1913) (holding that a subcontractor in a state with lower pay rates than New York was not required to pay the rates set in the New York statute).

36. *See* N.Y. Constitution art. 12, sec. 1 (now art. 13, sec. 14).

37. *See* People ex rel. Williams Engineering & Contracting Co. v. Metz, 193 N.Y. 148 (1908). *But cf.* People v. Phyfe, 136 N.Y. 554 (1893), where the court of appeals refused to enforce hours legislation by means of a criminal prosecution under a statute in which the legislature had set maximum hours but had not explicitly stated that violation of the maximum hours provision constituted a crime.

38. *See* People v. C. Klinck Packing Co., 214 N.Y. 121 (1915).

39. *See* People v. New York Central R.R. Co., 148 N.Y. Supp. 495 (3d Dept. 1914).

40. *See* Ewen v. Thompson-Starrett Co., 208 N.Y. 245 (1913).

41. 189 N.Y. 131 (1907).

42. 189 N.Y. at 137.

43. 198 U.S. 45 (1905).

44. 189 N.Y. at 135–137.

45. *See* People ex rel. Hoelderlin v. Kane, 139 N.Y. Supp. 350 (Sup. Ct. Kings Co. 1913), *aff'd*, 146 N.Y. Supp. 1105 (2d Dept. 1914).

46. 208 U.S. 412 (1908).

47. 139 N.Y. Supp. at 352.

48. 139 N.Y. Supp. at 357.

Chapter 3. Business Law

1. *See* Morton J. Horwitz, *The Transformation of American Law, 1870–1960: The Crisis of Legal Orthodoxy* (New York: Oxford University Press, 1992), 36, 44–45.

2. Horwitz, *Transformation of American Law, 1870–1960*, 33.

3. *See* Horwitz, *Transformation of American Law, 1870–1960*, 34.

4. *See* William E. Nelson, *The Common Law in Colonial America: Volume I: The Chesapeake and New England, 1607–1660* (New York: Oxford University Press, 2008), 23–47.

5. *See generally* Morton J. Horwitz, *The Transformation of American Law, 1780–1860* (Cambridge, Mass.: Harvard University Press, 1977); James Willard Hurst, *Law and the Conditions of Freedom in the Nineteenth-Century United States* (Madison: University of Wisconsin Press, 1956).

6. 51 N.Y. 476 (1873).

7. 51 N.Y. at 484.

8. 86 N.Y. 140 (1881).

9. 86 N.Y. at 148.

10. Horwitz, *Transformation of American Law, 1870–1960*, 36.

11. On the mid-century background of anti-monopoly law, *see* Watson v. Harlem & New York Navigation Co., 52 How. Pr. 348 (Sup. Ct. N.Y. Co. 1877). On the validity of special pretrial procedures in monopoly cases, *see* Matter of Davies, 168 N.Y. 89 (1901) (allowing attorney general to depose witnesses before filing suit).

12. Central New York Telephone & Telegraph Co. v. Averill, 199 N.Y. 128, 134 (1910). *Accord*, People v. North River Sugar Refining Co., 121 N.Y. 582 (1890).

13. Leslie v. Lorillard, 110 N.Y. 519, 533 (1888) (dictum).

14. 110 N.Y. at 533.

15. Unckles v. Colgate, 25 N.Y. Supp. 672, 675 (1st Dept. 1893), *aff'd*, 148 N.Y. 529 (1896).

16. Clancey v. Onondaga Fine Salt Mfg. Co., 62 Barb. 395, 403, 407 (Sup. Ct. 1862).

17. People v. Milk Exchange Ltd., 145 N.Y. 267, 272 (1895). *Accord*, Gray v. Oxnard Brothers Co., 13 N.Y. Supp. 86 (1st Dept. 1891). *But cf.* Castorland Milk & Cheese Co. v. Shantz, 179 N.Y. Supp. 131 (Sup. Ct. Lewis Co. 1919) (upholding legality of dairy company organized by dairy farmers).

18. Cohen v. Berlin & Jones Envelope Co., 166 N.Y. 292, 304 (1901).

19. *See* Metropolitan Opera Co. v. Hammerstein, 221 N.Y. 507 (1917). *Contra*, Peerless Pattern Co. v. Pictorial Review Co., 132 N.Y. Supp. 37 (1st Dept. 1911); People v. Klaw, 106 N.Y. Supp. 341 (Gen. Sess. N.Y. Co. 1907); New York Motion Picture Co. v. Universal Film Mfg. Co., 137 N.Y. Supp. 278 (Sup. Ct. N.Y. Co. 1912).

20. *See* Arnot v. Pittston & Elmira Coal Co., 68 N.Y. 558 (1877).

21. *See* People v. Duke, 44 N.Y. Supp. 336 (Gen. Sess. N.Y. Co. 1897). *But see* Locker v. American Tobacco Co., 106 N.Y. Supp. 115 (2d Dept. 1907), *aff'd*, 195 N.Y. 565 (1909).

22. *See* Central New York Telephone & Telegraph Co. v. Averill, 199 N.Y. 128 (1910).

23. *See* Sultan v. Star Co., 174 N.Y. Supp. 52 (Sup. Ct. Kings Co. 1919).

24. For a general statement of the law prohibiting monopolies and its limits, *see* People v. American Ice Co., 120 N.Y. Supp. 443 (Sup. Ct. N.Y. Co. 1909), which consists of a trial judge's instructions to a jury.

25. *See* Natl Harrow Co. v. E. Bement & Sons, 163 N.Y. 505 (1900), *aff'd*, Bement v. Natl Harrow Co., 186 U.S. 70 (1902).

26. *See* Tabor v. Hoffman, 118 N.Y. 30 (1889); Eastman Co. v. Reichenbach, 20 N.Y. Supp. 110 (Sup. Ct. Monroe Co. 1892), *aff'd*, 21 N.Y. Supp. 1143 (5th Dept. 1894). The courts would not grant monopoly protection, however, to a mere idea or scheme, unconnected with particular physical devices for carrying out that idea. Bristol v. Equitable Life Assurance Socy, 5 N.Y. Supp. 131, 132 (1st Dept. 1889), *aff'd*, 132 N.Y. 264 (1892).

27. *See* Straus v. American Publishers Assn, 193 N.Y. 496 (1908), *rev'd*, 231 U.S. 222 (1913); 174th Street & St. Nicholas Ave. Amusement Co. V. Maxwell, 169 N.Y. Supp. 895 (Sup. Ct. N.Y. Co. 1918).

28. Rafferty v. Buffalo City Gas Co., 56 N.Y. Supp. 288, 289 (1st Dept. 1899). *Cf.* United States Vinegar Co. v. Schlegel, 22 N.Y. Supp. 407, 410 (1st Dept. 1893), *aff'd*, 143 N.Y. 537 (1894) (corporation formed to protect shareholders against ruinous competition not an unlawful monopoly); New York Motion Picture Co. v. Universal Film Mfg. Co., 137 N.Y. Supp. 278 (Sup. Ct. N.Y. Co. 1912) (combination to diminish waste, give better service, and obtain better prices not an unlawful monopoly).

29. *See* Matter of Attorney General v. Interborough Metropolitan Co., 110 N.Y. Supp. 186 (1st Dept. 1908); Venner v. New York Central R.R. Co., 158 N.Y. Supp. 602 (Sup. Ct. Westchester Co. 1916), *aff'd*, 164 N.Y. Supp. 626 (2d Dept. 1917), *aff'd*, 226 N.Y. 583 (1919). *But cf.* Abbott v. Johnstown, Gloversville, and Kingsboro Horse R.R. Co., 80 N.Y. 27 (1880) (railroad company that leases road to individual still responsible for duties to public).

30. *See* Ives v. Smith, 8 N.Y. Supp. 46 (1st Dept. 1889).

31. *See* Brooklyn Elevated R.R. Co. v. Brooklyn, B. & W.E.R. Co., 48 N.Y. Supp. 665 (2d Dept. 1897). *Cf.* Venner v. New York Central R.R. Co., 143 N.Y. Supp. 211 (Sup. Ct. Albany Co. 1913) (approving exchange of equipment), *aff'd*, 145 N.Y. Supp. 725 (3d Dept. 1914), *aff'd*, 217 N.Y. 615 (1916). *But cf.* Talcott v. Wabash R.R. Co., 159 N.Y. 461 (1899) (connecting rail line not responsible for damage to passengers' luggage).

32. *See* Heim v. New York Stock Exchange, 118 N.Y. Supp. 591 (Sup. Ct. Kings Co. 1909), *aff'd*, 122 N.Y. Supp. 872 (2d Dept. 1910).

33. *See* Walsh v. Dwight, 58 N.Y. Supp. 91 (1st Dept. 1899).

34. *See* Export Lumber Co. v. South Brooklyn Sawmill Co., 67 N.Y. Supp. 626 (1st Dept. 1900).

35. 175 N.Y. 1 (1903).

36. 175 N.Y. at 14.

37. Hodge v. Sloan, 107 N.Y. 244, 249 (1887). *Accord*, Roseneau v. Empire Circuit Co., 115 N.Y. Supp. 511 (4th Dept. 1909). *Cf.* Collins v. American News Co., 69 N.Y. Supp. 638 (Sup. Ct. N.Y. Co. 1901), *aff'd*, 73 N.Y. Supp. 1123 (1st Dept. 1902) (parties may refuse to enter into contract with competing party).

38. Watertown Thermometer Co. v. Pool, 4 N.Y. Supp. 861, 864 (4th Dept. 1889).

39. 107 N.Y. at 249.

40. New York Bank-Note Co. v. Hamilton Bank-Note Engraving & Printing Co., 31 N.Y. Supp. 1060, 1062 (1st Dept. 1895). For other examples of cases upholding covenants not to compete, *see, e.g.*, Marsh v. Russell, 66 N.Y. 288 (1876); Roseneau v. Empire Circuit Co., 115 N.Y. Supp. 511 (4th Dept. 1909); Wilkinson Bros. & Co. v. Ebbets, 170 N.Y. Supp. 1041 (Sup. Ct. N.Y. Co. 1918). Sometimes covenants that disadvantaged "little fellows" were upheld. *See* Hoyt v. Fuller, 19 N.Y. Supp. 962 (Super. Ct. N.Y. City 1892).

41. Shakespeare v. Markham, 72 N.Y. 400, 403 (1878). *But see* Bell v. Smith, 32 N.Y. Supp. 54 (5th Dept. 1894) (age and feebleness do not necessarily render a person incompetent to manage their affairs).

42. *See* Mulderrig v. Burke, 53 N.Y. Supp. 1004 (App. Term 1898). *But cf.* Rozen v. Dry-Dock, E.B. & B.R. Co., 27 N.Y. Supp. 337 (Ct. Com. Pleas N.Y. Co. 1894) (literate employee who had capacity to understand unfavorable contract term bound thereby).

43. *See* Melle v. Candelora, 88 N.Y. Supp. 385 (App. Term 1904). *But cf.* Phillip v. Gallant, 62 N.Y. 256 (1875), where a woman who spoke

French was held to a contract whose terms had been explained to her in French.

44. *See* Recknagel v. Steinway, 69 N.Y. Supp. 132 (1st Dept. 1901). *But see* Doyle v. Rector of Trinity Church, 133 N.Y. 372 (1892) (laborer who agrees to work for free for New York City's largest landowner and completes work may not subsequently sue for wages).

45. *See* Frank V. Strauss & Co. v. Welsbach Gas Lamp Co., 85 N.Y. Supp. 367 (App. Term 1903).

46. *See* Devlin v. Smith, 89 N.Y. 470 (1882); Statler v. Ray Mfg. Co., 195 N.Y. 478 (1909) (dictum); MacPherson v. Buick Motor Co., 217 N.Y. 382 (1916). Early cases tended to reach the opposite result. *See* Loop v. Litchfield, 42 N.Y. 351 (1870) (manufacturer liable only for inherently dangerous but not normal products); Losee v. Clute, 51 N.Y. 494 (1873) (manufacturer even of dangerous product not liable to victim not in privity when purchaser tests product to his satisfaction and assumes control thereof). *Cf.* Priolo v. Southard Wrecking & Trucking Co., 198 N.Y. 528 (1910) (defendant that furnished defective machine liable to injured worker not in privity).

47. 184 N.Y. 379 (1906).

48. 184 N.Y. at 385.

49. American League Baseball Club of Chicago v. Chase, 149 N.Y. Supp. 6, 12 (Sup. Ct. Erie Co. 1914).

50. *See* Straus v. Cunningham, 144 N.Y. Supp. 1014 (1st Dept. 1913).

51. *See* Osborn v. Robbins, 36 N.Y. 365 (1867); Guilleaume v. Rowe, 94 N.Y. 268 (1883).

52. *See* Adams v. Irving Natl Bank, 116 N.Y. 606 (1889). *Contra*, Metropolitan Life Ins. Co. v. Meeker, 85 N.Y. 614 (1881); Knapp v. Hyde, 60 Barb. 80 (Sup. Ct. Monroe Co. 1869).

53. *See* Ingersoll v. Roe, 65 Barb. 346 (1st Dept. 1873); Maricle v. Brooks, 5 N.Y. Supp. 210 (4th Dept. 1889).

54. *See* Dunham v. Griswold, 100 N.Y. 224 (1885).

55. *See* Abelman v. Indelli & Conforti Co., 156 N.Y. Supp. 401 (1st. Dept. 1915).

56. *See* J.J. Little & Ives Co. v. Madison Paper Stock Co., 169 N.Y. Supp. 104 (1st Dept. 1918).

57. *See* Grabosski v. Gewerz, 17 N.Y. Supp. 528 (Ct. Com. Pleas N.Y. Co. 1892).

58. *See* Miller v. Curtiss, 15 N.Y. Supp. 140 (1st Dept. 1891), *aff'd*, 133 N.Y. 622 (1892); Spier v. Hyde, 87 N.Y. Supp. 285 (1st Dept. 1904).

59. *See* Adams v. Gillig, 199 N.Y. 314 (1910). For additional fraud cases, *see also* Barnes v. Brown, 80 N.Y. 527 (1880); Ritzwoller v. Lurie, 225 N.Y. 464 (1919); Greer v. Tweed, 13 Abb. Pr. N.S. 427 (Ct. Com. Pleas N.Y. City 1872). It did not matter if the false statement later turned out to be true. *See* Lehman-Charley v. Bartlett, 120 N.Y. Supp. 501 (1st Dept. 1909), *aff'd*, 202 N.Y. 524 (1911). Mere failure to disclose a fact did not, however, amount to fraud; explicit misstatement was required. *See* Rothmiller v. Stein, 143 N.Y. 581 (1894) (dictum).

60. *See* Prahar v. Tousey, 87 N.Y. Supp. 845 (2d Dept. 1904); Bystrom v. Villard, 162 N.Y. Supp. 100 (1st Dept. 1916).

61. *See* Summers v. Carey, 74 N.Y. Supp. 980 (2d Dept. 1902).

62. *See* Bliss v. Matteson, 45 N.Y. 22 (1871).

63. *See* John Weber & Co. v. Hearn, 63 N.Y. Supp. 41 (1st Dept. 1900).

64. *See* Nirdlinger v. Bernheimer, 35 N.Y. Supp. 807 (1st Dept. 1895), *aff'd*, 153 N.Y. 652 (1897).

65. *See* Hurwitz v. Hurwitz, 31 N.Y. Supp. 25 (Ct. Com. Pleas N.Y Co. 1894). *Cf.* Young v. Leach, 50 N.Y. Supp. 670 (1st Dept. 1898) (suit does not lie to recover damages for perjury occurring in suit to set aside fraudulent transfer).

66. *See* Manson v. Curtis, 223 N.Y. 313 (1918); Rosenthal v. Light, 227 N.Y. 587 (1919); Fabre v. ODonohue, 173 N.Y. Supp. 472 (2d Dept. 1918). Earlier lower court cases had reached a contrary result. *See* Scruggs v. Cotterill, 73 N.Y. Supp. 882 (1st Dept. 1902); Bonta v. Gridley, 78 N.Y. Supp. 961 (4th Dept. 1902).

67. *See* Ridgely v. Keene, 119 N.Y. Supp. 451 (2d Dept. 1909).

68. *See* Mills v. Mills, 40 N.Y. 543 (1869); Metz v. Woodward-Brown Realty Co., 169 N.Y. Supp. 299 (2d Dept. 1918).

69. *See* Veazey v. Allen, 173 N.Y. 359 (1903).

70. *See* Lyon v. Mitchell, 36 N.Y. 235 (1867); Southard v. Boyd, 51 N.Y. 177 (1872); Dunham v. Hastings Pavement Co., 68 N.Y. Supp. 221 (1st Dept. 1901).

71. *See* Chesebrough v. Conover, 140 N.Y. 382 (1893).

72. *See* Russell v. Burton, 66 Barb. 539 (Sup. Ct. St. Lawrence Co. 1867).

73. *See* Nickelson v. Wilson, 60 N.Y. 362 (1875).

74. *See* Randolph v. Stokes, 110 N.Y. Supp. 20 (2d Dept. 1908).

75. *See* Rhodes v. Stone, 17 N.Y. Supp. 561 (5th Dept. 1892).

76. N.Y. 239 (1921).

77. *See* Johnson v. De Peyster, 50 N.Y. 666 (1872); Phillip v. Gallant, 62

N.Y. 256 (1875); Woodward v. Fuller, 80 N.Y. 312 (1880); Flaherty v. Miner, 123 N.Y. 382 (1890); Spence v. Ham, 163 N.Y. 220 (1900) (dictum).

78. Leslie v. Lorillard, 110 N.Y. 519, 533 (1888) (dictum).

79. *See* Hooker v. Eagle Bank of Rochester, 30 N.Y. 83 (1864); New York, Providence & Boston R.R. Co. v. Dixon, 114 N.Y. 80 (1889); Leinkauf v. Lombard, 137 N.Y. 417 (1893); Sullivan County Club v. Butler, 56 N.Y. Supp. 1 (Sup. Ct. N.Y. Co. 1899). Any special assessments authorized by corporate bylaws to pay corporate debts were strictly construed. *See* Delaware Valley Telephone Co. v. Tiffany, 115 N.Y. Supp. 867 (3d Dept. 1909).

80. *See* Johnson v. Underhill, 52 N.Y. 203 (1873); Natl Tube Works Co. v. Gilfillan, 124 N.Y. 302 (1891); White Corbin & Co. v. Jones, 167 N.Y. 158 (1901); Bottlers Seal Co. v. Rainey, 225 N.Y. 369 (1919). This rule applied to banks as well as other types of corporations. *See* Matter of Reciprocity Bank, 22 N.Y. 9 (1860). When the stock was fully paid in, a certificate thereof was issued, but that certificate was not conclusive evidence of payment. *See* Veeder v. Mudgett, 95 N.Y. 295 (1884). A director of a corporation was not a creditor entitled to recover under this rule—*see* McDowell v. Sheehan, 129 N.Y. 200 (1891)—nor were shareholders of out-of-state corporations bound by the rule. *See* Southworth v. Morgan, 205 N.Y. 293 (1912).

81. *See* Wakefield v. Fargo, 90 N.Y. 213 (1882) (dictum). But an attorney employed by a corporation at a fixed salary was not considered a laborer. *See* Bristor v. Smith, 158 N.Y. 157 (1899).

82. Hastings v. Drew, 76 N.Y. 9, 16 (1879).

83. *See* Rorke v. Thomas, 56 N.Y. 559 (1874); Holmes v. Camp, 219 N.Y. 359 (1916). The prohibition on transfer of assets did not prohibit an officer of a corporation from selling his claim against the corporation. *See* Jefferson County Natl Bank v. Townley, 159 N.Y. 490 (1899). But a company that had failed to make a payment on any debt could not transfer any asset to a director who also was a creditor. *See* Throop v. Hatch Lithographic Co., 125 NY. 530 (1891).

84. *See* Booth v. Bunce, 33 N.Y. 139 (1865); Hastings v. Drew, 76 N.Y. 9 (1879). *Cf.* Natl Union Bank of Watertown v. Landon, 45 N.Y. 410 (1871) (shareholders who agree to put in extra money to continue business become partners fully liable for the business's debts).

85. Kavanaugh v. Kavanaugh Knitting Co., 226 N.Y. 185, 194 (1919).

86. 209 N.Y. 265 (1913). *Cf.* Hun v. Cary, 82 N.Y. 65 (1880) (directors of bank act as fiduciaries for depositors).

87. 209 N.Y. at 282.

88. *See* Kavanaugh v. Kavanaugh Knitting Co., 226 N.Y. 185 (1919). *Accord*, Schwab v. E.G. Potter Co., 194 N.Y. 409 (1909); Godley v. Crandall & Godley Co., 212 N.Y. 121 (1914).

89. *See* Butts v. Wood, 37 N.Y. 317 (1867). *But cf.* Young v. United States Mortgage & Trust Co., 214 N.Y. 279 (1915) (extra salary upheld on evidence of authorization by board and ratification by shareholders). When a shareholder became an officer without any agreement for a salary, the presumption was that he planned to work gratuitously. *See* Mather v. Eureka Mower Co., 118 N.Y. 629 (1890). But a person who was neither a director nor shareholder was entitled to reasonable compensation in the absence of an agreement. *See* Smith v. Long Island R.R. Co., 102 N.Y. 190 (1886).

90. *See* Gamble v. Queens County Water Co., 123 N.Y. 91 (1890).

91. *See* Billings v. Shaw, 209 N.Y. 265 (1913). *Accord*, Hinds v. Fishkill & Mattewan Equitable Gas Co., 88 N.Y. Supp. 954 (1st Dept. 1904).

92. *See* Blake v. Buffalo Creek R.R. Co., 56 N.Y. 485 (1874).

93. *See* Brinckerhoff v. Bostwick, 88 N.Y. 52 (1882).

94. *See* Brewster v. Hatch, 122 N.Y. 349 (1890); Heckscher v. Edenborn, 203 N.Y. 210 (1911); Downey v. Finucane, 205 N.Y. 251 (1912); Colton Improvement Co. v. Richter, 55 N.Y. Supp. 486 (Sup. Ct. Erie Co. 1890); Gray v. Heinze, 144 N.Y. Supp. 1045 (Sup. Ct. Monroe Co. 1913).

95. Getty v. Devlin, 54 N.Y. 403, 412 (1873).

96. *See* Jones v. Terre Haute & Richmond R.R. Co., 57 N.Y. 196 (1874) (dictum and dissenting opinion).

97. *See* Barr v. New York, Lake Erie & Western R.R. Co., 96 N.Y. 444 (1884). An important right that minority shareholders possessed entitled them to examine corporate books to watch for management misconduct. *See* Matter of Steinway, 159 N.Y. 250 (1899); Althause v. Giroux, 107 N.Y. Supp. 191 (App. Term 1907).

98. Hart v. Ogdensberg & L.C.R.R. Co., 35 N.Y. Supp. 566, 569 (3d Dept. 1895). *Accord*, Colby v. Equitable Trust Co. of New York, 108 N.Y. Supp. 978 (1st Dept.), *aff'd*, 192 N.Y. 535 (1908).

99. *See* Skinner v. Smith, 134 N.Y. 240 (1892); Continental Ins. Co. v. New York & Harlem R.R. Co., 187 N.Y. 225 (1907). *Cf.* Pollitz v. Wabash R.R. Co., 207 N.Y. 113 (1912) (suit barred when act of directors approved by majority of shareholders).

100. *See* Waters v. Horace Waters & Co., 201 N.Y. 184 (1911).

101. *See* Polhemus v. Polhemus, 95 N.Y. Supp. 325 (2d Dept. 1905), *rehearing granted*, 100 N.Y. Supp. 263 (2d Dept. 1906). *See also* Rothbart v.

Star Wet Wash Laundry Co., 174 N.Y. Supp. 76 (1st Dept. 1919) (suit dismissed for plaintiff's failure to indicate in what capacity he brought suit).

102. *See* Sheridan Elec. Light Co. v. Chatham Natl Bank, 127 N.Y. 517 (1891). But they could not set up a secret structure of control inconsistent with the law's formal structure, *see* Manson v. Curtis, 223 N.Y. 313 (1918), nor could officers or directors be removed from office without cause before the end of their terms. *See* People ex rel. Manice v. Powell, 201 N.Y. 194 (1911); Cuppy v. Stollwerck Bros. Inc., 216 N.Y. 591 (1916). *See also* Commercial Wood & Cement Co. v. Northampton Portland Cement Co., 190 N.Y. 1 (1907) (power of executive committee of board of directors suspended during hours immediately before meeting of full board).

103. *See* Beveridge v. New York Elevated R.R. Co., 112 N.Y. 1 (1889).

104. *See* Burden v. Burden, 159 N.Y. 287 (1899); Continental Ins. Co. v. New York & Harlem R.R. Co., 187 N.Y. 225 (1907).

105. *See* Kavanaugh v. Kavanaugh Knitting Co., 226 N.Y. 185 (1919); Mitchell v. Forest City Printing Co., 176 N.Y. Supp. 157 (3d Dept. 1919).

106. *See* Horwitz, *Transformation of American Law*, 1870–1960, 39–41, 44–45.

107. Globe & Rutgers Fire Ins. Co. v. Warner Sugar Refining Co., 176 N.Y. Supp. 3, 5 (1st Dept. 1919).

108. 34 N.Y. 30 (1865).

109. 34 N.Y. at 59–60, 70 (emphasis in original).

110. *See* Small v. Housman, 208 N.Y. 115 (1913).

111. *See* Hill v. Miller, 76 N.Y. 32 (1879).

112. *See* Globe & Rutgers Fire Ins. Co. v. Warner Sugar Refining Co., 176 N.Y. Supp. 3 (1st Dept. 1919).

113. *See* Sloss Iron & Steel Co. v. Jackson Architectural Ironworks, 92 N.Y. Supp. 1056 (1st Dept. 1905).

114. *See* Morrison v. Chapman, 140 N.Y. Supp. 700 (1st Dept. 1913).

115. *See* J.C. Bogert Co. v. Harpootlian, 132 N.Y. Supp. 367 (App. Term. 1911). For additional cases binding principals, *see* Bennett v. Judson, 21 N.Y. 238 (1860); Purcell v. Jaycox, 59 N.Y. 288 (1874); Edwards v. Dooley, 120 N.Y. 540 (1890); New York City Car Advertising Co. v. Morris Park Estates, 222 N.Y. 552 (1917). *But cf.* Crane v. Gruenewald, 120 N.Y. 274 (1890) (mortgage payment made to attorney who arranged loan is valid only if attorney is agent of mortgagee with authority to receive payment).

116. *See* Reis v. Drug & Chemical Club, 105 N.Y. Supp. 285 (App. Term 1907).

117. *See* Gilbert v. Deshon, 107 N.Y. 324 (1887).

118. *See* New York University v. Loomis Laboratory, 178 N.Y. 137 (1904). For additional cases declining to bind alleged principals, *see* McGoldrick v. Willits, 52 N.Y. 612 (1873); Conklin v. Mitchell, 57 N.Y. 650 (1874); Saugerties & N.Y. Steamboat Co. v. Miller, 78 N.Y. Supp. 451 (3d Dept. 1902); Hoffman v. American Tobacco Co., 148 N.Y. Supp. 151 (1st Dept. 1914).

119. *See* Figueira v. Lerner, 65 N.Y. Supp. 293 (2d Dept. 1900).

120. *See* Walsh v. Hartford Fire Ins. Co., 73 N.Y. 5 (1878); Bickford v. Menier, 107 N.Y. 490 (1887).

121. *See* Porges v. United States Mortgage & Trust Co., 203 N.Y. 181 (1911); Commonwealth Trust Co. v. Young, 107 N.Y. Supp. 555 (1st Dept. 1907).

122. *See* Gill v. Jamaica Bay Mfg. Co., 157 N.Y. Supp. 52 (2d Dept. 1916).

123. *See* Nicoll v. Burke, 78 N.Y. 580 (1879); Gotthelf v. Shapiro, 210 N.Y. 538 (1913). *But see* Peterson v. City of New York, 194 N.Y. 437 (1909) (undisclosed principal cannot enforce contract made by agent under seal). *See also* Elliott v. Brady, 192 N.Y. 221 (1908) (only parties to sealed contract can bring suit thereupon).

124. *See* Kelly Asphalt Block Co. v. Barber Asphalt Paving Co., 211 N.Y. 68 (1914).

125. *See* Ludwig v. Gillespie, 105 N.Y. 653 (1887).

126. *See* Wright v. Cabot, 89 N.Y. 570 (1882).

127. *See* Georgi v. Texas Co., 225 N.Y. 410 (1919). For suits against the principal, *see* Jessup v. Steurer, 75 N.Y. 613 (1878); Kayton v. Barnett, 116 N.Y. 625 (1889). For suits against the agent, *see* Pond v. Clark, 57 N.Y. 653 (1874); Cobb v. Knapp, 71 N.Y. 348 (1877); Laska v. Harris, 215 N.Y. 554 (1915).

128. *See* Meeker v. Claghorn, 44 N.Y. 349 (1871).

129. *See* Price v. Keyes, 62 N.Y. 378 (1875) (dictum); Weyerhauser v. Dun, 100 N.Y. 150 (1885).

130. *See* Fifth Ave. Bank v. Forty-Second St. & Grand St. Ferry R.R. Co., 137 N.Y. 231 (1893); Jarvis v. Manhattan Beach Co., 148 N.Y. 652 (1896); Green v. des Garets, 210 N.Y. 79 (1913); Laska v. Harris, 215 N.Y. 554 (1915).

131. Yeoman v. McClenahan, 190 N.Y. 121, 127–128 (1907). *But see* Henry v. Wilkes, 37 N.Y. 562 (1868) (mortgagor not liable when agent absconds with money borrowed to pay off mortgage); Mali v. Lord, 39 N.Y. 381 (1868) (principal not liable for willful injury committed by agent unless authorized by principal).

Chapter 4. Personal Injury Law

1. *See* John Fabian Witt, *The Accidental Republic: Crippled Workingmen, Destitute Widows, and the Remaking of American Law* (Cambridge, MA: Harvard University Press, 2004), 2–3. This estimate is derived from a study of accidents in Colorado.

2. *See* Randolph E. Bergstrom, *Courting Danger: Injury and Law in New York City, 1870–1910* (Ithaca, NY: Cornell University Press, 1992), 17, 20; Witt, *Accidental Republic*, 59.

3. Elon R. Brown, *Some Faults of Legal Administration*, in New York State Bar Association, *Proceedings of the Thirty-First Annual Meeting Held at New York, January 21, 24–25, 1908* (1908), 136, 142.

4. Reynolds v. New York Central R.R. Co., 58 N.Y. 248, 250–251 (1874). *Accord*, Grippen v. New York Central R.R. Co., 40 N.Y. 34 (1869). *Cf.* Scaggs v. Delaware & Hudson Canal Co., 145 N.Y. 201 (1895) (dismissed on finding of no negligence on part of defendant).

5. Magar v. Hammond, 171 N.Y. 377, 383 (1902); McLean v. Studebaker Bros. Co., 221 N.Y. 475 (1917).

6. *See* Morris v. Lake Shore & Michigan Southern Ry. Co., 148 N.Y. 182, 186 (1896).

7. Hale v. Smith, 78 N.Y. 480, 483 (1879).

8. *See* Hart v. Hudson River Bridge Co., 84 N.Y. 56 (1881).

9. Curran v. Warren Chemical & Mfg. Co., 36 N.Y. 153, 155 (1867) (dictum).

10. *See* Vykess v. Duncan Co., 84 N.Y. Supp. 398 (3d Dept. 1903).

11. Savage v. Nassau Elec. R, R. Co., 59 N.Y. Supp. 225, 229 (2d Dept. 1899), *aff'd*, 168 N.Y. 680 (1901).

12. Murphy v. Hayes, 145 N.Y. 370, 375 (1895). *Cf.* Dalzell v. New York, N.H. & H. R.R. Co., 121 N.Y. Supp. 28 (2d Dept. 1910) (no recovery for plaintiff since accident caused by fellow servant, not third-party defendant); Connelly v. Rist, 45 N.Y. Supp. 321 (Sup. Ct. N.Y. Co. 1897) (ibid.).

13. *See* Hoffman v. King, 160 N.Y. 618, 628 (1899); Trapp v. McClellan, 74 N.Y. Supp. 130, 132 (2d Dept. 1902); Restivo v. Conklin, 157 N.Y. Supp. 627, 629 (2d Dept. 1916).

14. *See* Murphy v. City of New York, 85 N.Y. Supp. 445 (1st Dept. 1903).

15. *See* McGovern v. Degnon-McLean Contracting Co., 105 N.Y. Supp. 408 (2d Dept. 1907); Ryan v. Cortland Carriage Goods Co., 118 N.Y. Supp. 56 (3d Dept. 1909); Davy v. Lyons, 127 N.Y. Supp. 1083 (App. Term 1911).

16. 158 N.Y. 73 (1899).

17. 158 N.Y. at 99.

18. Von Wangenheim v. New York Stockyards Co., 153 N.Y. Supp. 696, 697 (Sup. Ct. N.Y. Co.), *aff'd*, 155 N.Y. Supp. 405 (1st Dept. 1915) (dictum).

19. *See* Hall v. New York Telephone Co., 214 N.Y. 49 (1915).

20. *See* Cleary v. Blake, 43 N.Y. Supp. 1115 (2d Dept. 1897).

21. *See* Miller v. Bahmmuller, 108 N.Y. Supp. 924 (2d Dept. 1908).

22. *See* Von Wangenheim v. New York Stockyards Co., 153 N.Y. Supp. 696 (Sup. Ct. N.Y. Co.), *aff'd*, 155 N.Y. Supp. 405 (1st Dept. 1915).

23. *See* Heffernan v. Arnold, 63 N.Y. Supp. 261 (3d Dept. 1900).

24. Generally the issue whether an injury was foreseeable was one for the jury. *See* Daly v. J. M. Horton Ice Cream Co., 151 N.Y. Supp. 657, 659 (2d Dept. 1915).

25. *See* Ship v. Fridenberg, 117 N.Y. Supp. 599 (1st Dept. 1909). *Cf.* Silverblatt v. Brooklyn Telegraph & Messenger Co., 134 N.Y. Supp. 765 (2d Dept. 1912) (burglar alarm company not liable for value of stolen goods when alarm failed during course of burglary).

26. *See* Pardington v. Abraham, 87 N.Y. Supp. 670 (2d Dept. 1904), *aff'd*, 183 N.Y. 553 (1906).

27. 158 N.Y. 73 (1899).

28. *See* Land v. New York Central R.R. Co., 227 N.Y. 507 (1920), *aff'd*, 255 U.S. 455 (1921).

29. *See* Victory v. Baker, 67 N.Y. 366 (1876); Walsh v. Fitchburg R.R. Co., 145 N.Y. 301 (1895); Birch v. City of New York, 190 N.Y. 397 (1907); Connell v. New York Central R.R. Co., 129 N.Y. Supp. 666 (2d Dept. 1911).

30. *See* Hart v. Grennell, 122 N.Y. 371 (1890) (dictum).

31. *See* Cleveland v. New Jersey Steamboat Co., 68 N.Y. 306 (1877) (dictum).

32. *See* Dougherty v. D.C. Weeks & Son, 111 N.Y. Supp. 218 (1st Dept. 1908) (dictum).

33. Cosulich v. Standard Oil Co., 122 N.Y. 118, 123 (1890). *Accord*, Kirby v. President of Delaware & H. Canal Co., 62 N.Y. Supp. 1110 (3d Dept. 1900), *aff'd*, 169 N.Y. 575 (1901); Loeber v. Roberts, 17 N.Y. Supp. 378 (Super Ct. N.Y. City 1892), *aff'd*, 138 N.Y. 606 (1893).

34. Parsan v. Johnson, 208 N.Y. 337, 343 (1913).

35. *See* Green v. Urban Contracting & Heating Co., 94 N.Y. Supp. 743 (1st Dept. 1905).

36. *See* Hitchcock v. Riley, 89 N.Y. Supp. 890 (Sup. Ct. Franklin Co. 1904).

37. *See* Fitzgerald v. Rodgers, 68 N.Y. Supp. 946 (1st Dept. 1901).

38. *See* Hanna v. Pitt & Scott, 106 N.Y. Supp. 145 (2d Dept. 1907).

39. *See* Filiponne v. Reisenburger, 119 N.Y. Supp. 632 (2d Dept. 1909).

40. *See* Bergstrom, *Courting Danger*, 158.

41. 43 N.Y. 502 (1871).

42. 9 N.Y. Supp. 104 (1st Dept. 1890).

43. 9 N.Y. Supp. at 105.

44. *See* Steinacker v. Hills Bros. Co., 87 N.Y. Supp. 33 (2d Dept. 1904); Spannknebel v. New York Central R.R., 111 N.Y. Supp. 705 (2d Dept. 1908).

45. *See* Kunz v. City of Troy, 104 N.Y. 344 (1887); Schmidt v. Cook, 23 N.Y. Supp. 799 (Com. Pleas N.Y. Co. 1893), *revg*, 20 N.Y. Supp. 889 (City Ct. N.Y. City 1892).

46. *See* McKay v. Syracuse Rapid Transit Ry. Co., 208 N.Y. 359 (1913).

47. *See* McCormack v. Nassau Elec. R.R. Co., 46 N.Y. Supp. 230 (2d Dept. 1897); Harper v. Delaware, L. & W.R.R. Co., 47 N.Y. Supp. 933 (3d Dept. 1897); Hobson v. New York Condensed-Milk Co., 49 N.Y. Supp. 209 (2d Dept. 1898). *See also* Cleghorn v. New York Central R.R. Co., 56 N.Y. 44 (1874) (holding that a railroad could be liable for punitive damages for an accident resulting from the negligence of a drunken employee if the official who hired and retained the employee knew of his bad habits).

48. Seaman v. Koehler, 122 N.Y. 646, 648 (1890).

49. 99 N.Y. 158 (1885).

50. 99 N.Y. at 162.

51. 66 N.Y. 50 (1876).

52. 66 N.Y. at 53.

53. Hartman v. Berlin & Jones Envelope Co., 127 N.Y. Supp. 187, 188 (Sup. Ct. Kings Co.), *aff'd*, 131 N.Y. Supp. 1119 (2d Dept. 1911).

54. *See* Mertz v. Connecticut Co., 217 N.Y. 475 (1916); Munger v. Baker, 65 Barb. 539 (4th Dept. 1873); Fitzpatrick v. Garrison & West Point Ferry Co., 1 N.Y. Supp. 794 (2d Dept. 1888); Albee v. Chappaqua Shoe Mfg. Co., 16 N.Y. Supp. 687 (2d Dept. 1891); Hankins v. Watkins, 28 N.Y. Supp. 867 (4th Dept. 1894); Newell v. Woolfolk, 36 N.Y. Supp. 327 (2d Dept. 1895); Williams v. Koehler, 58 N.Y. Supp. 863 (2d Dept. 1899); Ramsey v. Natl Contracting Co., 63 N.Y. Supp. 286 (2d Dept. 1900); Francis C. Neale, Inc. v. New York Steam Co., 132 N.Y. Supp. 71 (1st Dept. 1911).

55. *See* Briggs v. New York Central R.R. Co., 72 N.Y. 26 (1878); Knupfle v. Knickerbocker Ice Co., 84 N.Y. 488 (1881); Acton v. Reid, 93 N.Y. Supp. 911 (1st Dept. 1905). An owner would not be liable, however, for an injury

resulting from some cause other than breach of the statute. *See* Koch v. Fox, 75 N.Y. Supp. 913 (1st Dept. 1902); Kuhnen v. White, 92 N.Y. Supp. 104 (2d Dept. 1905).

56. 78 N.Y. 310 (1879).

57. 78 N.Y. at 314.

58. 173 N.Y. 530 (1903).

59. 173 N.Y. at 535–536.

60. Shields v. Paul B. Pugh & Co., 107 N.Y. Supp. 604, 606 (1st Dept. 1907).

61. 201 N.Y. 240 (1911).

62. 201 N.Y. at 244–245.

63. 210 N.Y. 252 (1914).

64. 214 N.Y. 531 (1915). *Cf.* People v. Harris, 134 N.Y. Supp. 409 (Gen. Sess. N.Y. Co. 1911) (upholding manslaughter indictment charging culpable negligence for locking doors in Triangle Waist Company in violation of statute resulting in deaths of employees in fire, noting, however, that whether the deaths resulted from the negligence was in a criminal case a question of fact for the jury).

65. 214 N.Y. at 534–535.

66. 214 N.Y. at 535–536.

67. *See* Ursprung v. Winter Garden Co., 169 N.Y. Supp. 738 (1st Dept. 1918); Flynt v. Rightmeyer, 177 N.Y. Supp. 842 (Sup. Ct. Orange Co. 1919).

68. 228 N.Y. 164 (1920).

69. 228 N.Y. at 168–170 (emphasis in original).

70. Mullen v. St. John, 57 N.Y. 567, 571 (1874). *Contra*, Odell v. Solomon, 99 N.Y. 635 (1885). *Cf.* Herman v. City of Buffalo, 214 N.Y. 316 (1915) (owner of building not liable for negligent failure of contractor to construct building in accordance with proper plans).

71. *See* Breen v. New York Central R.R. Co., 109 N.Y. 297 (1888).

72. *See* Griffen v. Manice, 166 N.Y. 188 (1901) (dictum).

73. *See* McNulty v. Ludwig & Co., 138 N.Y. Supp. 84 (2d Dept. 1912).

74. *See* Kaufman v. Hopper, 220 N.Y. 184 (1917).

75. *See* Webster v. Hudson River R.R. Co., 38 N.Y. 260 (1868).

76. *See* Bergstrom, *Courting Danger*, 159.

77. *See* Robert J. Kaczorowski, "From Petitions for Gratuities to Claims for Damages: Personal Injuries and Railroads during the Industrialization of the United States," *American Journal of Legal History* 57 (2017): 261.

78. Witt, *Accidental Republic*, 71–72. Witt examines the cooperative insurance movement in detail at 71–102.

79. Charles Richard Van Hise, *The Conservation of Natural Resources in the United States* (New York: Macmillan, 1910), 364, 369–370.

80. *See* Witt, *Accidental Republic*, 114.

81. E. M. Atkin and H. M. Edwards, *Compensation to Injured Employees: Plan of the New York Edison Company* (New York: Association of Edison Illuminating Companies, 1910), 5.

82. *See* Bergstrom, *Courting Danger*, 141–142.

83. Eli Shelby Hammond, "Personal Injury Litigation," *Yale Law Journal* 6 (1897): 330.

84. Samuel S. Page, "Personal Injury Actions: The Defendants Standpoint," *Illinois Law Review* 1 (1906): 27, 29.

85. *See* text at notes 55–69, *supra*.

86. *See* N.Y. Laws of 1902, ch. 600.

87. *See* N.Y. Laws of 1902, ch. 600, sec. 1.

88. *See* N.Y. Laws of 1902, ch. 600, sec. 3. *See generally* Bergstrom, *Courting Danger*, 74–75.

89. *See* N.Y. Laws of 1906, ch. 657.

90. *See* Bergstrom, *Courting Danger*, 77.

91. *See* N.Y. Laws of 1910, ch. 674.

92. *See* Witt, *Accidental Republic*, 127.

93. 201 N.Y. 271 (1911).

94. Lyman v. Putnam Coal & Ice Co., 169 N.Y. Supp. 984, 987 (2d Dept. 1918), *aff'd*, 230 N.Y. 548 (1920).

95. *See* N.Y. Constitution, art. 1, sec. 19 (now section 18).

96. *See* N.Y. Laws of 1914, ch. 41. *See generally* Witt, *Accidental Republic*, 176.

97. 215 N.Y. 514 (1915).

98. *See* Southern Pacific Co. v. Jensen, 244 U.S. 205 (1917). *See also* Schumacher v. Pennsylvania R.R. Co., 175 N.Y. Supp. 84 (Sup. Ct. Erie Co. 1919) (refusing to hold unconstitutional congressional legislation allowing tort suits against railroads for injuries occurring while railroads were under federal control during World War I).

Chapter 5. The Law of Pleading and Civil Procedure

1. N.Y. Laws of 1848, ch. 379, secs. 62 and 120. *See also* N.Y. Laws of 1849, ch. 349 and N.Y. Laws of 1850, ch. 281 (amendments to 1848 code).

2. Alger v. Scoville, 6 How. Pr. 131, 144 (Sup. Ct. 1851).

3. Le Roy v. Marshall, 8 How. Pr. 373, 376 (Sup. Ct. Dutchess Co. 1853).

4. Shaw v. Jayne, 4 How. Pr. 119, 121 (Sup. Ct. N.Y. Co. 1849).

5. Dollner v. Gibson, 2 Edm. Sel. Cas. 253, 253 (Sup. Ct. N.Y. Co. 1850).

6. Wooden v. Waffle, 6 How. Pr. 145, 148 (Sup. Ct. Monroe Co. 1851).

7. Boyce v. Brown, 7 Barb. 80, 87 (Sup. Ct. St, Lawrence Co. 1849).

8. Boyce v. Brown, 7 Barb. 80, 84–85 (Sup. Ct. St. Lawrence Co. 1849) (emphasis in original).

9. 7 Barb. at 85–86.

10. Dollner v. Gibson, 2 Edm. Sel. Cas. 253, 254–255 (Sup. Ct. N.Y. Co. 1850).

11. Knowles v. Gee, 8 Barb. 300, 301–302 (Sup. Ct. N.Y. Co. 1850) (emphasis in original). See also Shaw v. Jayne, 4 How. Pr. 119 (Sup. Ct. N.Y. Co. 1849).

12. 2 Edm. Sel. Cas. at 254–255.

13. See Exner v. Exner, 2 Abb. N. Cas. 108 (1st Dept. 1876); Halbe v. Adams, 158 N.Y. Supp. 380 (1st Dept. 1916); Hendrix v. Manhattan Beach Dev. Co., 168 N.Y. Supp. 316 (1st Dept. 1917); Sheldon v. Lake, 40 How. Pr. 489 (Com. Pl. N.Y. Co. 1871).

14. Masterson v. Short, 35 How. Pr. 169, 170–171 (Super. Ct. 1868).

15. 5 How. Pr. 470 (Sup. Ct. Rensselaer Co. 1851).

16. 5 How. Pr. at 473–474.

17. 5 How. Pr. 272 (Sup. Ct. Erie Co. 1850)

18. 5 How. Pr. 216 (Sup. Ct. Monroe Co. 1851).

19. 5 How. Pr. at 219 (emphasis in original).

20. 5 How. Pr. at 220.

21. 5 How. Pr. at 221–222 (emphasis in original).

22. 5 How. Pr. at 222.

23. See Wooden v. Waffle, 6 How. Pr. 145 (Sup. Ct. Monroe Co. 1851). Accord, Knowles v. Gee, 4 How. Pr. 317 (Sup. Ct. Wayne Co. 1850).

24. See Shaw v. Jayne, 4 How. Pr. 119 (Sup. Ct. N.Y. Co. 1849); Alger v. Scoville, 6 How. Pr. 131 (Sup. Ct. 1851); Minor v. Terry, 6 How. Pr. 208 (Sup. Ct. 1851); Le Roy v. Marshall, 8 How. Pr. 373 (Sup. Ct. Dutchess Co. 1853).

25. For equity cases in which facts were pleaded in detail, see Meyers v. City of New York, 69 N.Y. Supp. 529 (1st Dept. 1901); Pullman v. Mayor of City of New York, 49 Barb. 57 (Sup. Ct. 1866), revd on other grounds, 54 Barb. 169 (General Term 1869); Bertha Zinc & Mineral Co. v. Clute, 27 N.Y. Supp. 342 (Com. Pl. N.Y. Co. 1894). But see Masterson v. Short, 35 How. Pr. 169, 170–171 (Super. Ct. 1868), where plaintiff's counsel argued that only issuable facts needed to be pleaded but cited Knowles v. Gee, 4 How. Pr. 317 (Sup. Ct. 1850), which agreed with Justice Selden.

26. *See* Reubens v. Joel, 13 N.Y. 488 (1856); Linden v. Hepburn, 5 How. Pr. 188 (Super. Ct. 1850). *Cf.* Alger v. Scoville, 6 How. Pr. 131 (Sup. Ct. 1851), which prohibited joinder of cases in different categories, a prohibition described by the court as "mainly an embodiment of the rules of pleading as they existed" prior to the code. 6 How. Pr. at 140. Inconsistent claims also could not be joined. *See* Mayo v. Knowlton, 134 N.Y. 250 (1892).

27. Gould v. Cayuga County Nat'l Bank, 86 N.Y. 75, 83 (1881).

28. 22 N.Y. 225 (1860).

29. 22 N.Y. at 228.

30. 86 N.Y. 75, 82 (1881).

31. *See* Moser v. Cochrane, 107 N.Y. 35 (1887).

32. *See* Hunt v. Chapman, 51 N.Y. 555 (1873); Parsons v. Sutton, 66 N.Y. 92 (1876); Hull v. Hull, 225 N.Y. 342 (1919). A counterclaim could not be brought under this approach if it had not matured at the time the promissory note that was the subject of the action was assigned by the holder to the plaintiff who brought suit. *See* Martin v. Kunzmuller, 37 N.Y. 396 (1867).

33. Kelly v. Webster, 128 N.Y. Supp. 58, 60 (4th Dept. 1911).

34. Seibert v. Dunn, 216 N.Y. 237, 245 (1915). *See also* Goodman v. Benjamin Rutchik, Inc., 171 N.Y. Supp. 152 (2d Dept. 1918) (doctrines of setoff and recoupment governed by counterclaim rules).

35. *See* Dunn v. Uvalde Asphalt Paving Co., 175 N.Y. 214 (1903).

36. *See* Carpenter v. Manhattan Life Ins. Co., 93 N.Y. 552 (1883).

37. *See* Taylor v. Mayor of City of New York, 83 N.Y. 625 (1881).

38. *See* Kelley v. Webster, 128 N.Y. Supp. 58 (4th Dept. 1911).

39. 93 N.Y. at 556–557. For another case reaching the same result on the same theory, *see* Thomson v. Sanders, 118 N.Y. 252 (1890). For cases holding that counterclaims did not arise out of the same transaction as the initial suit and hence could not be filed, *see* Fulton County Gas & Elec. Co. v. Hudson River Telephone Co., 200 N.Y. 287 (1911); Morris v. Windsor Trust Co., 213 N.Y. 27 (1914); Lundine v. Callaghan, 81 N.Y. Supp. 1052 (2d Dept. 1903).

40. *See* Cragin v. Lovell, 88 N.Y. 258 (1882) (dictum).

41. *See* Pond v. Harwood, 139 N.Y. 111 (1893); Richard Deeves & Son v. Manhattan Life Ins. Co., 195 N.Y. 324 (1909).

42. *See* Dunham v. Bower, 77 N.Y. 76 (1879).

43. *See* United States Trust Co. v. Stanton, 139 N.Y. 531 (1893). *Cf.* Mowry v. Peet, 88 N.Y. 453 (1882) (judgment cannot be rendered against estate upon counterclaim by personal representatives).

44. *See* Baitzel v. Rhinelander, 167 N.Y. Supp. 343 (1st Dept. 1917).

45. *See* N.Y. Laws of 1831, ch. 300, sec. 1.

46. 1 Hill 225 (Sup. Ct. 1841).

47. 7 Hill 182 (Sup. Ct. 1845).

48. *See* Miller v. Scherder, 2 N.Y. 262 (1849).

49. 6 N.Y. 560 (1852). *See also* Field v. Morse, 7 How. Pr. 12 (Sup. Ct. Monroe Co. 1852) and 8 How. Pr. 47 (Sup. Ct. Monroe Co. 1853) (holding it inappropriate to include allegations of fraud in complaint for purposes of obtaining defendant's arrest and allowing amendment of complaint to remove them).

50. *See* Smith v. Knapp, 30 N.Y. 581 (1864); Elwood v. Gardner, 45 N.Y. 349 (1871); Moffatt v. Fulton, 132 N.Y. 507 (1892). *But cf.* Fenton v. Duckworth, 115 N.Y. Supp. 686 (2d Dept. 1909) (arrest and imprisonment not available in equity action).

51. *See* McDonald v. Metropolitan St. Ry. Co., 167 N.Y. 66 (1901); Hagan v. Sone, 174 N.Y. 317 (1903); Wynn v. Provident Life & Trust Co. of Philadelphia, 206 N.Y. 701 (1912). For examples of cases appropriately submitted to juries, *see* Froelich v. City of New York, 199 N.Y. 466 (1910); Queeney v. Willi, 225 N.Y. 374 (1919).

52. Maxwell v. G.H. Peters Co., 219 N.Y. 597, 598 (1916).

53. Colt v. Sixth Ave. R.R. Co., 49 N.Y. 671, 671 (1872).

54. *See* Howell v. Adams, 68 N.Y. 314 (1877).

55. Lyman v. Putnam Coal & Ice Co., 169 N.Y. Supp. 984, 986 (2d Dept. 1918), *aff'd*, 230 N.Y. 548 (1920).

56. Westervelt v. Phelps, 171 N.Y. 212 (1902).

57. Cothran v. Collins, 29 How. Pr. 155, 167–168 (Sup. Ct. Erie Co. 1865). *Accord*, Brush v. Constable, 152 N.Y. Supp. 20 (2d Dept. 1915); Howley v. Kraemer, 73 N.Y. Supp. 142 (App. Term 1901); Edelson v. Monahan, 126 N.Y. Supp. 583 (App. Term 1911); Tatum v. Tatum, 151 N.Y. Supp. 448 (Sup. Ct. Nassau Co. 1915).

58. 29 How. Pr. at 170.

59. *See* Jarchover v. Dry-Dock, E.B. & B.R.R. Co., 66 N.Y. Supp. 575 (1st Dept. 1900); Hong v. Brooks, 164 N.Y. Supp. 388 (Sup. Ct. Monroe Co. 1917).

60. *See* Romaine v. Village of Spring Valley, 105 N.Y. Supp. 256 (2d Dept. 1907).

61. Nichols v. Sixth Ave. R.R. Co., 38 N.Y. 131, 135 (1868).

62. Girshoff v. Marx, 124 N.Y. Supp. 1083, 1084 (2d Dept. 1910).

63. Grogan v. Brooklyn Heights R.R. Co., 95 N.Y. Supp. 23, 24 (2d

Dept. 1905). *Accord*, Zunino v. Parodi Cigar Co., 174 N.Y. Supp. 524 (1st Dept. 1919).

64. Munday v. Nassau Elec. R.R. Co., 163 N.Y. Supp. 508, 510 (Sup. Ct. Kings Co. 1917).

65. Cox v. Halloran, 81 N.Y. Supp. 803, 806 (2d Dept. 1903).

66. 163 N.Y. Supp. at 510. *Accord*, Odell v. Webendorfer, 69 N.Y. Supp. 930 (2d Dept. 1901); Goldberg v. Burrows, 172 N.Y. Supp. 761 (1st Dept. 1918); Schwartz v. Joline, 111 N.Y. Supp. 726 (App. Term 1908). *See also* Nolan v. Harris, 52 How. Pr. 409 (Sup. Ct. N.Y. Co. 1876) (verdict should not be set aside when only nominal damages at stake). *Accord*, Garrison v. Sun Printing & Publishing Ass'n, 150 N.Y. Supp. 284 (1st Dept. 1914); Rosenthal v. Jacob Dold Packing Co., 171 N.Y. Supp. 76 (App. Term 1918). When damages were excessive, one remedy was to not grant a new trial but issue a remittur reducing damages. *See* Pesant v. Metropolitan St. Ry. Co., 89 N.Y. Supp. 314 (1st Dept. 1904); Quirk v. Siegel-Cooper Co., 56 N.Y. Supp. 49 (Sup. Ct. Kings Co.), *aff'd*, 60 N.Y. Supp. 228 (2d Dept. 1899). But a new trial could be awarded when there was no proper basis for reducing the verdict as a condition of denying the motion for a new trial. Abrashkov v. Ryan, 114 N.Y. Supp. 973, 974 (1st Dept. 1909). For other cases granting new trials because of excessive damages, *see* Fawdrey v. Brooklyn Heights R.R. Co., 72 N.Y. Supp. 283 (2d Dept. 1901); Ross v. Metropolitan St. Ry. Co., 93 N.Y. Supp. 679 (1st Dept. 1905).

67. *See* Voisin v. Commercial Mutual Ins. Co., 70 N.Y. Supp. 147 (1st Dept 1901); Buttner v. City of New York, 97 N.Y. Supp. 303 (1st Dept. 1905); White v. Robinson, 138 N.Y. Supp. 932 (1st Dept. 1912); Napoli v. Erie R.R. Co., 165 N.Y. Supp. 206 (1st Dept. 1917); Schuster v. Arscott, 110 N.Y. Supp. 1107 (App. Term 1908).

68. *See* Algeo v. Duncan, 39 N.Y. 313 (1868); Specht v. Waterbury Co., 208 N.Y. 374 (1913); Pangburn v. Buick Motor Co., 211 N.Y. 228 (1914); Deyo v. Hudson, 225 N.Y. 602, *rehearing denied*, 226 N.Y. 685 (1919); Hutchins v. Rutland R.R. Co., 148 N.Y. Supp. 397 (3d Dept. 1914). *Cf.* Sherman v. Delaware, Lackawanna & Western R.R. Co., 106 N.Y. 542 (1887) (new trial granted because of admission of incompetent evidence).

69. Mack v. Hines, 184 N.Y. Supp. 152, 154 (Sup. Ct. Kings Co. 1920).

70. Bigelow v. Garwitz, 15 N.Y. Supp. 940, 940 (5th Dept. 1891).

71. O'Shea v. McLear, 1 N.Y. Supp. 407, 408 (3d Dept. 1888). *Accord*, McDonald v. Walter, 40 N.Y. 551 (1869); De La Torre v. Metropolitan St. Ry. Co., 62 N.Y. Supp. 604 (1st Dept. 1900); Milliken v. City of New

York, 81 N.Y. Supp. 866 (2d Dept. 1903); Goodwin v. The Ansonia, 173 N.Y. Supp. 194 (1st Dept. 1918).

72. *See* Lorch v. Lorch, 63 N.Y. Supp. 567 (1st Dept. 1900); Peterson v. Eighmie, 161 N.Y. Supp. 1065 (1st Dept. 1916); Bardar v. Perrazzo, 157 N.Y. Supp. 886 (App. Term 1916).

73. *See* Lamour v. Northern Iron Co., 148 N.Y. Supp. 458 (3d Dept. 1914); Hoffman v. New York Ry. Co., 147 N.Y. Supp. 900 (City Ct. N.Y. City 1914). *But cf.* Eustis v. Steinson, 84 N.Y. Supp. 155 (App. Term 1903) (denying new trial for contempt of court by opposing litigant).

74. *See* Peyser v. Coney Island & B.R.R. Co., 30 N.Y. Supp. 610 (1st Dept. 1894); Popadinec v. Manhattan Ry. Co., 96 N.Y. Supp. 913 (2d Dept. 1905); Ballard v. Village of Hamburg, 128 N.Y. Supp. 325 (4th Dept. 1911). For denials of such motions, *see* Sayer v. King, 47 N.Y. Supp. 422 (2d Dept. 1897); Lane v. Brooklyn Heights R.R. Co., 82 N.Y. Supp. 1057 (2d Dept. 1903).

75. *See* People v. Glasgow, 52 N.Y. Supp. 24 (3d Dept. 1898); Pratt v. Burns, 177 N.Y. Supp. 817 (3d Dept. 1919).

76. Azzara v. Nassau Elec. R.R. Co., 118 N.Y. Supp. 830, 832 (2d Dept. 1909).

77. 154 N.Y. Supp. 12 (Sup. Ct. Queens Co. 1915).

78. 154 N.Y. Supp. at 14.

79. 86 N.Y. 75 (1881).

80. 86 N.Y. at 85–86.

Chapter 6. The Law of Nuisance

1. *See* Campbell v. Seaman, 63 N.Y. 568 (1876).

2. *See* Cogswell v. New York, New Haven & Hartford R.R. Co., 103 N.Y. 10 (1886).

3. Leonard v. Spencer, 108 N.Y. 338 (1888).

4. Bohan v. Port Jervis Gaslight Co., 122 N.Y. 18 (1890). *Cf.* Booth v. Rome, Watertown & Ogdensburg Terminal R.R. Co., 140 N.Y. 267 (1893) (dictum) (defendant should use least intrusive measures to accomplish appropriate work).

5. 189 N.Y. 40 (1907).

6. 189 N.Y. at 44.

7. 189 N.Y. at 50 (1907).

8. 208 N.Y. 1 (1913).

9. 208 N.Y. at 4.

10. 208 N.Y. at 5–6.

11. For other nuisance cases in the court of appeals granting injunctions, *see* Cranford v. Tyrrell, 128 N.Y. 341 (1891) (enjoining house of prostitution); Davis v. Niagara Falls Tower Co., 171 N.Y. 336 (1902) (enjoining owner of tower not to permit ice to form on it in winter); Barnes v. Midland R.R. Terminal Co., 193 N.Y. 378 (1908) (granting new trial to enjoin obstruction of public's right to walk along beach). For cases involving only damages, *see* Jutte v. Hughes, 67 N.Y. 267 (1876) (flooding of plaintiffs' premises caused by improper maintenance of privies and drains); Hogle v. H. H. Franklin Mfg. Co., 199 N.Y. 388 (1910) (articles thrown at plaintiff from neighbor's window). For cases limiting the damages that plaintiffs could recover, *see* Pond v. Metropolitan Elevated Ry. Co., 112 N.Y. 186 (1889); Barrick v. Schifferdecker, 123 N.Y. 52 (1890).

12. *See* Morgan v. City of Binghamton, 102 N.Y. 500 (1886); Lester v. Mayor of City of New York, 29 N.Y. Supp. 1000 (1st Dept. 1894), *aff'd*, 150 N.Y. 578 (1896). Lower courts, however, were sometimes willing to enjoin municipal activities. *See* Kobbe v. Village of New Brighton, 45 N.Y. Supp. 777 (Sup. Ct. Kings Co.), *aff'd*, 48 N.Y. Supp. 990 (2d Dept. 1897) (enjoining burning of garbage); Bohnsack v. McDonald, 56 N.Y. Supp. 347 (Sup. Ct. N.Y. Co. 1899) (use of methods not contemplated by legislature enjoined).

13. *See* Benner v. Atlantic Dredging Co., 134 N.Y. 156 (1892).

14. *See* Bremer v. Manhattan Ry. Co., 191 N.Y. 333 (1908).

15. McCarty v. Natural Carbonic Gas Co., 189 N.Y. 40, 46–47 (1907). *Accord*, Murphy v. Leggett, 164 N.Y. 121 (1900).

16. *See* Filson v. Crawford, 5 N.Y. Supp. 882 (Sup. Ct. N.Y. Co. 1889) (dictum).

17. Spring v. Delaware, L. & W.R.R. Co., 34 N.Y. Supp. 810 (4th Dept. 1895), *aff'd*, 157 N.Y. 692 (1898).

18. *See* Pach v. Geoffroy, 22 N.Y. Supp. 275 (1st Dept. 1893), *aff'd*, 143 N.Y. 661 (1894); Friedman v. Columbia Machine Works & Malleable Iron Co., 91 N.Y. Supp. 129 (2d Dept. 1904); Ereon v. Niagara Steel Finishing Co., 166 N.Y. Supp. 442 (Sup. Ct. Niagara Co. 1917); Mulligan v. Elias, 12 Abb. Pr. N.S. 259 (City Ct. Brooklyn 1872).

19. *See* Ricker v. Shaler, 85 N.Y. Supp. 825 (2d Dept. 1903).

20. *See* Rosenheimer v. Standard Gaslight Co., 55 N.Y. Supp. 192 (1st Dept. 1898).

21. *See* Pritchard v. Edison Elec. Illuminating Co., 87 N.Y. Supp. 225 (1st Dept.), *aff'd*, 179 N.Y. 364 (1904).

22. *See* Braender v. Harlem Lighting Co., 2 N.Y. Supp. 245 (Sup. Ct. N.Y. Co. 1888).

23. *See* Dunsbach v. Hollister, 2 N.Y. Supp. 94 (3d Dept. 1888), *aff'd*, 132 N.Y. 602 (1892).

24. *See* Morgan v. Bowes, 17 N.Y. Supp. 22 (1st Dept. 1891); Gordon v. Village of Silver Creek, 112 N.Y. Supp. 54 (4th Dept. 1908), *aff'd*, 197 N.Y. 509 (1909). For other nuisance cases decided in favor of plaintiffs, *see* Olmsted v. Rich, 6 N.Y. Supp. 826 (4th Dept. 1889); United States Illuminating Co. v. Grant, 7 N.Y. Supp. 788 (1st Dept. 1889); Barnard v. Finkbeiner, 147 N.Y. Supp. 514 (2d Dept. 1914).

25. *See* Hochstrasser v. Martin, 26 N.Y. Supp. 410 (3d Dept. 1893); Stillwell v. Buffalo Riding Academy, 4 N.Y. Supp. 414 (Sup. Ct. N.Y. Co. 1888).

26. *See* Herrlich v. New York Central R.R. Co., 126 N.Y. Supp. 311 (Sup. Ct. N.Y. Co. 1910).

27. *See* Butterfield v. Klaber, 52 How. Pr. 255 (Super. Ct. 1877).

28. *See* Knaub v. Meyer, 141 N.Y. Supp. 819 (Sup. Ct. Kings Co. 1913).

29. *See* Roscoe Lumber Co. v. Standard Silica Cement Co., 70 N.Y. Supp. 1130 (2d Dept. 1901); American Ice Co. v. Catskill Cement Co., 90 N.Y. Supp. 801 (3d Dept. 1904); Bentley v. Empire Portland Cement Co., 96 N.Y. Supp. 831 (Sup. Ct. Onondaga Co. 1905).

30. *See* Orr v. Baltimore & Ohio R.R. Co., 153 N.Y. Supp. 920 (1st Dept. 1915). *Cf.* Cibulski v. Hutton, 62 N.Y. Supp. 166 (3d Dept. 1900) (reversing jury's finding of nuisance because of improper instruction).

31. *See* Lee v. Vacuum Oil Co., 7 N.Y. Supp. 426 (5th Dept. 1889).

32. *See* De Moll v. City of New York, 148 N.Y. Supp. 966 (2d Dept. 1914).

33. *See* People v. Transit Dev. Co., 115 N.Y. Supp. 297 (2d Dept. 1909); Farrell v. New York Steam Co., 53 N.Y. Supp. 55 (Sup. Ct. N.Y. Co. 1898).

34. *See* Gunning System v. City of Buffalo, 71 N.Y. Supp. 155 (4th Dept. 1901).

35. *See* Whitridge v. Calestock, 165 N.Y. Supp. 640 (1st Dept. 1917).

36. *See* Leonard v. Hotel Majestic Co., 40 N.Y. Supp. 1044 (Sup. Ct. N.Y. Co. 1896).

37. *See* Doellner v. Tynan, 38 How. Pr. 176 (Super. Ct. 1869).

38. *See* Sommers Mercantile Co. v. Rheinfrank House Wrecking Co., 113 N.Y. Supp. 402 (Sup. Ct. N.Y. Co. 1908).

39. *See* Kushes v. Ginsburg, 91 N.Y. Supp. 216 (1st Dept. 1904), *aff'd*, 188 N.Y. 630 (1907).

40. *See* Piehl v. Albany Ry., 51 N.Y. Supp. 755 (3d Dept. 1898), *aff'd*, 162 N.Y. 617 (1900).

41. *See* Depierris v. Mattern, 10 N.Y. Supp. 626 (Sup. Ct. N.Y. Co. 1890).

42. *See* Sandmann v. Baylies, 47 N.Y. Supp. 783 (City Ct. N.Y. City 1897), *aff'd*, 56 N.Y. Supp. 1070 (App. Term 1899).

43. *See* Riedeman v. Mt. Morris Elec. Light Co., 67 N.Y. Supp. 391 (1st Dept. 1900); Peck v. Newburgh Light, Heat & Power Co., 116 N.Y. Supp. 433 (2d Dept. 1909); Beauchamp v. Excelsior Brick Co. of Haverstraw, 127 N.Y. Supp. 686 (2d Dept. 1911); Newbold v. Childs Co., 132 N.Y. Supp. 366 (1st Dept. 1911); De Carvajal v. Young Men's Christian Ass'n of City of New York, 76 N.Y. Supp. 474 (Sup. Ct. N.Y. Co. 1902).

44. 21 Abb. N. Cas. 159 (Sup. Ct. N.Y. Co. 1888).

45. 21 Abb. N. Cas. at 161, 163.

46. 154 N.Y. Supp. 96 (Sup. Ct. Kings Co. 1915), *aff'd*, 158 N.Y. Supp. 1117 (2d Dept. 1916).

47. 154 N.Y. Supp. at 96.

48. 116 N.Y. Supp. 46 (1st Dept. 1909).

49. 116 N.Y. Supp. at 47–48.

Chapter 7. Religion and Morality

1. Lindenmuller v. People, 33 Barb. 548, 561–562 (Sup. Ct. 1861).

2. 33 Barb. at 568.

3. 33 Barb. at 574.

4. 33 Barb. at 569–570.

5. *See* Silverberg Brothers v. Douglass, 114 N.Y. Supp. 824 (Sup. Ct. Erie Co. 1909).

6. Matter of Agudath Hakehiloth, 42 N.Y. Supp. 985, 986 (Sup. Ct. N.Y. Co. 1896).

7. 33 Barb. at 574–575.

8. *See* Lindenmuller v. People, 33 Barb. 548 (Sup. Ct. 1861).

9. *See* People v. Moses, 140 N.Y. 214 (1893).

10. *See* People v. Ebbets, 172 N.Y. Supp. 599 (Spec. Sess. Kings Co. 1917).

11. Holcombe v. Leavitt, 124 N.Y. Supp. 980, 981 (Sup. Ct. Erie Co. 1910) (dictum). *Accord*, Connitt v. Reformed Protestant Dutch Church of New Prospect, 54 N.Y. 551, 561 (1874).

12. *See* Connitt v. Reformed Protestant Dutch Church of New Prospect, 54 N.Y. 551 (1874); Bristor v. Burr, 120 N.Y. 427 (1890); Conway v. Carpenter, 30 N.Y. Supp. 315 (2d Dept. 1894); Rector of St. James Church v. Huntington, 31 N.Y. Supp. 91 (4th Dept. 1894); Robinson v. Cocheu, 46 N.Y. Supp. 55 (2d Dept. 1897); Burrel v. Associate Reformed Church of Town of Seneca, 44 Barb. 282 (Sup. Ct. 1865); Isham v. Fullager, 14 Abb. N. Cas. 363 (Sup. Ct. N.Y. Co. 1881); Isham v. Trustees of First Presbyterian Church of Dunkirk, 63 How. Pr. 465 (Sup. Ct. N.Y. Co. 1882). *Cf.* Parshley v. Third Methodist Episcopal Church in Brooklyn, 147 N.Y. 583 (1895) (church leaders could also employ other individuals to do church business).

13. 155 N.Y. 83 (1898).

14. 155 N.Y. at 98–99.

15. *See* Smith v. Bowers, 68 N.Y. Supp. 169 (3d Dept. 1901), *aff'd*, 171 N.Y. 669 (1902); McGuire v. St. Patrick's Cathedral, 3 N.Y. Supp. 781 (Sup. Ct. N.Y. Co.), *aff'd*, 7 N.Y. Supp. 345 (1st Dept. 1889); Waller v. Howell, 45 N.Y. Supp. 790 (Sup. Ct. Orange Co. 1897).

16. *See* Watkins v. Wilcox, 66 N.Y. 654 (1876); White v. Miller, 71 N.Y. 118 (1877); St. Jacobs Lutheran Church of Town of Eden v. Bly, 73 N.Y. 323 (1878); Matter of First Presbyterian Society of Buffalo, 106 N.Y. 251 (1887). But an unauthorized conveyance of land would be invalidated. *See* Madison Avenue Baptist Church v. Baptist Church in Oliver Street, 46 N.Y. 131 (1871); Madison Avenue Baptist Church v. Baptist Church in Oliver Street, 73 N.Y. 82 (1878). In case of a schism, a legislative enactment was required to divide the church property between the two emerging congregations; courts had no jurisdiction to make the division. *See* Reformed Church of Gallupville v. Schoolcraft, 65 N.Y. 134 (1875).

17. *See* Burke v. Rector of Trinity Church, 117 N.Y. Supp. 255 (Sup. Ct. N.Y. Co.), *aff'd*, 117 N.Y. Supp. 1130 (1st Dept. 1909).

18. *See* Peoples Bank v. St. Anthony's Roman Catholic Church, 109 N.Y. 512 (1888). It was essential that governing authorities be sued in their proper capacity. *See* Davis v. First Congregational Society of Syracuse, 65 N.Y. 278 (1875).

19. Many cases construed the instruments pursuant to which property had been donated to churches. *See* People v. Rector of Trinity Church, 22 N.Y. 44 (1860); Levy v. Levy, 33 N.Y. 97 (1865); Attorney General ex rel. Marselus v. Dutch Reformed Protestant Church of New York, 36 N.Y. 452 (1867); Church of Redemption v. Grace Church, 68 N.Y. 570 (1877); Matter of Congregational Church & Society of Cutchogue, 131

N.Y. 1 (1892); First Presbyterian Church of Waterford v. McKallor, 54 N.Y. Supp. 740 (3d Dept. 1898); Washburn v. Acome, 131 N.Y. Supp. 963 (Sup. Ct. Saratoga Co. 1911), *aff'd*, 136 N.Y. Supp. 1150 (3d Dept. 1912); Matter of Collier, 97 Misc. 543 (Surr. Ct. Columbia Co. 1916), *aff'd*, 165 N.Y. Supp. 1081 (3d Dept. 1917).

20. *See* Petty v. Tooker, 21 N.Y. 267 (1860); Gram v. Prussia Emigrated Evangelical Lutheran German Society, 36 N.Y. 161 (1867).

21. *See* N.Y. Laws of 1875, ch. 79, sec. 4.

22. *See* N.Y. Laws of 1876, ch. 110, sec. 1.

23. *See* Westminster Presbyterian Church of West Twenty-Third Street v. Presbytery of New York, 211 N.Y. 214 (1914); Presbytery of New York v. Westminster Presbyterian Church of West Twenty-Third Street, 222 N.Y. 305 (1918); Application of Lloyds Memorial Congregational Church, 178 N.Y. Supp. 104 (Sup. Ct. Erie Co. 1919).

24. *See* People v. Tuthill, 31 N.Y. 550, 561–562 (1864); People ex rel. Lauchantin v. Lacoste, 37 N.Y. 192 (1867).

25. 110 N.Y. 33 (1888).

26. 110 N.Y. at 38.

27. Lindenmuller v. People, 33 Barb. 548, 567 (Sup. Ct. 1861).

28. 33 Barb. at 563–564.

29. 33 Barb. at 574.

30. 33 Barb. at 564.

31. *See* People v. Molling, 154 N.Y. Supp. 877 (Ct. Gen. Sess. N.Y. Co. 1915); People v. Berger, 169 N.Y. Supp. 319 (Ct. Gen. Sess. N.Y. Co. 1918).

32. *See* Dunn v. People, 29 N.Y. 523 (1864); People v. Vedder, 98 N.Y. 630 (1885).

33. People v. Deschessere, 74 N.Y. Supp. 761, 762 (1st Dept. 1902).

34. People ex rel. Lee v. Bixby, 67 Barb. 221 (1st Dept. 1875).

35. 163 N.Y. Supp. 680 (Sup. Ct. Kings Co. 1916) and 163 N.Y. Supp. 682 (Sup. Ct. Kings Co. 1917).

36. 163 N.Y. Supp. at 683–684.

37. 163 N.Y. Supp. at 681.

38. 163 N.Y. Supp. at 686.

39. People v. Doris, 43 N.Y. Supp. 571 (1st Dept.), *appeal dism.*, 153 N.Y. 678 (1897).

40. 43 N.Y. Supp. at 572.

41. 43 N.Y. Supp. at 573.

42. 96 N.Y. 408 (1884).

43. 96 N.Y. at 410–411.

44. People v. Tylkoff, 212 N.Y. 197 (1914).

45. *See* Hodecker v. Stricker, 46 N.Y. Supp. 808 (4th Dept. 1897).

46. Shepard v. Lamphier, 146 N.Y. Supp. 745, 746 (Sup. Ct. Erie Co. 1914).

47. *See* People v. Danahy, 18 N.Y. Supp. 467 (5th Dept. 1892); People v. Hallenbeck, 52 How. Pr. 502 (Sup. Ct. Greene Co. 1876).

48. People v. Kaufman, 43 N.Y. Supp. 1046, 1046 (1st Dept. 1897).

49. 188 N.Y. 478 (1907).

50. 188 N.Y. at 482–483.

51. 188 N.Y. at 479.

52. Levey v. Levey, 150 N.Y. Supp. 610, 611 (Sup. Ct. Kings Co. 1914), *aff'd*, 153 N.Y. Supp. 1125 (2d Dept. 1915).

53. Richardson v. Richardson, 114 N.Y. Supp. 912, 917 (Sup. Ct. Kings Co. 1906).

54. Evenden v. Evenden, 170 N.Y. Supp. 458, 459 (Sup. Ct. Broome Co. 1918).

55. *See* Caujolle v. Ferrie, 23 N.Y. 90 (1861); Hynes v. McDermott, 82 N.Y. 41 (1880); Badger v. Badger, 88 N.Y. 546 (1882); Hynes v. McDermott, 91 N.Y. 451 (1883); Gall v. Gall, 114 N.Y. 109 (1889); Ziegler v. P. Cassidy's Sons, 220 N.Y. 98 (1917); Matter of Brush, 49 N.Y. Supp. 803 (1st Dept. 1898); Davidson v. Ream, 164 N.Y. Supp. 1037 (3d Dept. 1917); Bissell v. Bissell, 55 Barb. 325 (Sup. Ct. 1869). A common-law marriage would not be found, however, if the parties merely agreed to live together without agreeing to live as husband and wife. *See* Harbeck v. Harbeck, 102 N.Y. 714 (1886); Soper v. Halsey, 33 N.Y. Supp. 105 (5th Dept. 1895).

56. *See* Taylor v. Taylor, 71 N.Y. Supp. 411 (1st Dept. 1901), *aff'd*, 173 N.Y. 266 (1903); Summo v. Snare & Triest Co., 152 N.Y. Supp. 29 (2d Dept. 1915); Donohue v. Donohue, 116 N.Y. Supp. 241 (Sup. Ct. Erie Co. 1909). *But see* Earle v. Earle, 126 N.Y. Supp. 317 (1st Dept. 1910) (enforcing statute granting spouse a right to seek an annulment in such a case).

57. 108 N.Y. Supp. 13 (2d Dept. 1908).

58. The unwillingness to disturb the marriage relation was evidenced by a refusal of one court to grant a divorce when a husband committed adultery several years after his wife left him because she had ceased to love him and would not live with a man she did not love, Richardson v. Richardson, 114 N.Y. Supp. 912, 914 (Sup. Ct. Kings Co. 1906), and by the requirement that suits for divorce had to be brought within five years of the first discovery of a spouse's adultery. *See* Ackerman v. Ackerman, 200 N.Y. 72 (1910).

59. Keville v. Keville, 106 N.Y. Supp. 993 (2d Dept. 1907). *Accord*, Smith v. Smith, 35 N.Y. Supp. 556 (3d Dept. 1895).

60. *See* Pollock v. Pollock, 71 N.Y. 137 (1877).

61. *See* Fontana v. Fontana, 170 N.Y. Supp. 308 (1st Dept. 1918).

62. *See* Beadleston v. Beadleston, 2 N.Y. Supp. 809 (1st Dept. 1888).

63. Conger v. Conger, 82 N.Y. 603, 603 (1880).

64. Glaser v. Glaser, 73 N.Y. Supp. 284, 284 (Sup. Ct. N.Y. Co. 1901).

65. *See* Mott v. Mott, 38 N.Y. Supp. 261 (1st Dept. 1896).

66. Jayne v. Jayne, 25 N.Y. Supp. 810, 811 (Super. Ct. N.Y. City 1893).

67. *See* Di Lorenzo v. Di Lorenzo, 174 N.Y. 467 (1903).

68. *See* Svenson v. Svenson, 178 N.Y. 54 (1904).

69. *See* Sobol v. Sobol, 150 N.Y. Supp. 248 (Sup. Ct. N.Y. Co. 1914).

70. *See* Jones v. Brinsmade, 183 N.Y. 258 (1905) (by implication); Farnham v. Farnham, 227 N.Y. 155 (1919) (by implication).

71. *See* Fontana v. Fontana, 135 N.Y. Supp. 220 (Sup. Ct. N.Y. Co. 1912).

72. *See* Stokes v. Stokes, 198 N.Y. 301 (1910).

73. *See* Cunningham v. Cunningham, 206 N.Y. 341 (1912); Mitchell v. Mitchell, 117 N.Y. Supp. 671 (Sup. Ct. Erie Co. 1909).

74. *See* Bays v. Bays, 174 N.Y. Supp. 212 (Sup. Ct. Cortland Co. 1918). *Cf.* Williams v. Williams, 130 N.Y. Supp. 875 (Sup. Ct. Oneida Co. 1911) (defendant lied about his age).

75. Hatch v. Hatch, 110 N.Y. Supp. 18, 18 (Sup. Ct. Erie Co. 1908).

76. *See* Wendel v. Wendel, 52 N.Y. Supp. 72 (2d Dept. 1898).

77. Schroter v. Schroter, 106 N.Y. Supp. 22, 22 (Sup. Ct. N.Y. Co. 1907).

78. *See* Shrady v. Logan, 40 N.Y. Supp. 1010 (Sup. Ct. N.Y. Co. 1896).

79. *See* Hoffman v. Hoffman, 46 N.Y. 30 (1871); ODea v. ODea, 101 N.Y. 23 (1885); De Meli v. De Meli, 120 N.Y. 485 (1890); Williams v. Williams, 130 N.Y. 193 (1891); Winston v. Winston, 165 N.Y. 553 (1901), *aff'd*, 189 U.S. 506 (1903); Munson v. Munson, 14 N.Y. Supp. 692 (3d Dept. 1891); McGowan v. McGowan, 43 N.Y. Supp. 745 (Sup. Ct. N.Y. Co. 1896), *aff'd*, 46 N.Y. Supp. 285 (1st Dept. 1897), *aff'd*, 164 N.Y. 558 (1900). New York courts also would not interfere with efforts to annul another state's judgment of divorce. *See* Guggenheim v. Wahl, 203 N.Y. 390 (1911). They did, however, uphold out-of-state divorces when both parties resided in the out-of-state jurisdiction at the time of the divorce. *See* In re Denick's Estate, 36 N.Y. Supp. 518 (4th Dept. 1895); Miller v. Miller, 128 N.Y. Supp. 787 (Sup. Ct. N.Y. Co. 1911). *See also* Atherton v. Atherton, 181 U.S. 155 (1901), *rev'g* 155 N.Y. 129 (1898) (upholding out-of-state decree when couple resided in that state until defendant moved to New York following

breakup of the marriage); Matter of Hall, 70 N.Y. Supp. 406 (3d Dept. 1901) (upholding out-of-state divorce when plaintiff resided in Dakota, never left the state after her divorce, and husband resided in Argentina).

80. *See* People v. Baker, 76 N.Y. 78 (1879).

81. 48 Barb. 566 (Sup. Ct. 1867). *Accord*, Van Voorhis v. Brintnall, 86 N.Y. 18 (1881); Thorp v. Thorp, 90 N.Y. 602 (1882); Moore v. Hegeman, 92 N.Y. 521 (1883); Matter of Eichler, 146 N.Y. Supp. 846 (Surr. Ct. N.Y. Co. 1914).

82. 48 Barb. at 567.

83. Silberstein v. Silberstein, 218 N.Y. 525, 529 (1916) (dictum).

84. *See* De Brauwere v. De Brauwere, 203 N.Y. 460 (1911). *See also* Winter v. Winter, 191 N.Y. 462 (1908), which upheld a provision for support contained in a separation agreement. Earlier cases had held such agreements invalid, *see* Poillon v. Poillon, 61 N.Y. Supp. 582 (Sup. Ct. N.Y Co. 1899), *aff'd*, 63 N.Y. Supp. 301 (1st Dept. 1900), unless the support money was paid through the medium of a trustee. *See* Clark v. Fosdick, 118 N.Y. 7 (1889). A woman could rescind a separation agreement as unfair if it provided inadequate support. *See* Hungerford v. Hungerford, 161 N.Y. 550 (1900), but a woman was not entitled to support if she left her husband to move in with her parents. *See* Catlin v. Martin, 69 N.Y. 393 (1877).

85. *See* Bennett v. Bennett, 116 N.Y. 584 (1889); Cochran v. Cochran, 111 N.Y. Supp. 588 (2d Dept. 1908), *revd on other grounds*, 196 N.Y. 86 (1909); Heermance v. James, 47 Barb. 120 (Sup. Ct. 1866). For a suit to be successful, it was necessary to prove more than that the defendant had improper relations with the guilty spouse; it was necessary to show that the defendant was the pursuer, and not merely the pursued. Buchanan v. Foster, 48 N.Y. Supp. 732, 733 (1st Dept. 1897). *Accord*, Hanor v. Housel, 113 N.Y. Supp. 163 (3d Dept. 1908).

86. Gray v. Gray, 148 N.Y. Supp. 1064, 1065–1066 (Sup. Ct. N.Y. Co. 1914).

87. Ruckman v. Ruckman, 58 How. Pr. 278, 279 (Sup. Ct. N.Y. Co. 1880). *Accord*, Waltermire v. Waltermire, 110 N.Y. 183 (1888); McBride v. McBride, 9 N.Y. Supp. 827 (1st Dept. 1890); Kissam v. Kissam, 47 N.Y. Supp. 270 (2d Dept. 1897); Kinsey v. Kinsey, 124 N.Y. Supp. 30 (Sup. Ct. Westchester Co. 1910); Rebstock v. Rebstock, 144 N.Y. Supp. 289 (Sup. Ct. Erie Co. 1913).

88. Morris v. Morris, 177 N.Y. Supp. 600, 601 (Sup. Ct. Kings Co. 1919). *Accord*, Fitzpatrick v. Fitzpatrick, 47 N.Y. Supp. 737 (Sup. Ct. N.Y. Co. 1897).

89. *See* Straus v. Straus, 22 N.Y. Supp. 567 (3d Dept. 1893); Smith v. Smith, 87 N.Y. Supp. 137 (1st Dept. 1904); De Meli v. De Meli, 67 How. Pr. 20, 32–33 (Sup. Ct. N.Y. Co. 1884) (dictum), *aff'd*, 120 N.Y. 485 (1890).

90. *See* Snyder v. Snyder, 162 N.Y. Supp. 607 (Sup. Ct. Monroe Co. 1917).

91. *See* Sheldon v. Sheldon, 131 N.Y. Supp. 291 (2d Dept. 1911).

92. *See* Abramowitz v. Abramowitz, 140 N.Y. Supp. 275 (Sup. Ct. Kings Co. 1913) (dictum).

93. *See* Barber v. Barber, 153 N.Y. Supp. 256 (2d Dept. 1915).

94. *See, e.g.*, People ex rel. Sinclair v. Sinclair, 86 N.Y. Supp. 539 (1st Dept. 1904).

95. *See* Osterhoudt v. Osterhoudt, 62 N.Y. Supp. 529 (1st Dept. 1900), *appeal dism.*, 168 N.Y. 358 (1901); People ex rel. Winston v. Winston, 72 N.Y. Supp. 456 (1st Dept. 1901). *See also* Baylis v. Baylis, 207 N.Y. 446 (1913), which left custody of a child of a second marriage, adjudged to be void because of an invalid divorce of a first marriage, in the hands of the mother, with a declaration that because the second marriage was void the child was illegitimate.

96. *See* Van Buren v. Van Buren, 78 N.Y. Supp. 23 (3d Dept. 1902); Lester v. Lester, 165 N.Y. Supp. 187 (2d Dept.), *aff'd*, 222 N.Y. 546 (1917).

97. *See* Ullman v. Ullman, 135 N.Y. Supp. 1080 (2d Dept. 1912).

98. *See* Kennedy v. Kennedy, 73 N.Y. 369 (1878); Erkenbrach v. Erkenbrach, 96 N.Y. 456 (1884); Galusha v. Galusha, 138 N.Y. 272 (1893); Hayes v. Hayes, 220 N.Y. 596 (1917); Levy v. Levy, 133 N.Y. Supp. 1084 (1st Dept. 1912); Wendling v. Wendling, 134 N.Y. Supp. 55 (Sup. Ct. N.Y. Co. 1912); Gilbert v. Gilbert, 26 N.Y. Supp. 30 (Ct. Com. Pleas N.Y. Co. 1893).

99. Gibson v. Gibson, 143 N.Y. Supp. 37, 40 (Sup. Ct. Erie Co. 1913). New York courts were not obligated to enforce support orders issued by out-of-state courts. *See* Lynde v. Lynde, 162 N.Y. 405 (1900), *aff'd*, 181 U.S. 183 (1901). *See also* Waring v. Waring, 100 N.Y. 570 (1885) (court has no jurisdiction to grant alimony in case of husband obtaining a separation decree in his favor).

100. *See* Wetmore v. Wetmore, 162 N.Y. 503 (1900); Kiralfy v. Kiralfy, 73 N.Y. Supp. 708 (Sup. Ct. N.Y. Co. 1901).

101. *See* Cowles v. Cowles, 51 N.Y. Supp. 1057 (1st Dept. 1898).

102. *See* N.Y Laws of 1848, ch. 200.

103. *See* N.Y. Laws of 1849, ch. 375.

104. *See* N.Y. Laws of 1860, ch. 90.

105. Abbey v. Deyo, 44 N.Y. 343, 348 (1871) (concurring opinion).

106. *See* Gage v. Dauchy, 34 N.Y. 293 (1866). The same was true of property acquired by a husband from his father-in-law before the 1848 act, which property he declared belonged to her. *See* Syracuse Chilled Plow Co. v. Wing, 85 N.Y. 421 (1881). *Accord*, Woodworth v. Sweet, 51 N.Y. 8 (1872).

107. *See* Stevens v. Cunningham, 181 N.Y. 454 (1905).

108. *See* Sammis v. McLaughlin, 35 N.Y. 647 (1866).

109. *See* Sherman v. Elder, 24 N.Y. 381 (1862).

110. *See* Buckley v. Wells, 33 N.Y. 518 (1865); Abbey v. Deyo, 44 N.Y. 343 (1871).

111. *See* Bitter v. Rathman, 61 N.Y. 512 (1875).

112. *See* Ballin v. Dillaye, 37 N.Y. 35 (1867); Herrington v. Robertson, 71 N.Y. 280 (1877).

113. *See* Ackley v. Westervelt, 86 N.Y. 448 (1881).

114. Coleman v. Burr, 93 N.Y. 17, 24–25 (1883). *Cf.* Tallinger v. Mandeville, 113 N.Y. 427 (1889) (holding illegal a man's ante-nuptial agreement to pay a wife $10,000 for faithfully performing her duties as a wife until his death but permitting her to retain the $5,000 that had been paid).

115. Birkbeck v. Ackroyd, 74 N.Y. 356, 358–359 (1878).

116. *See* Reynolds v. Robinson, 64 N.Y. 589 (1876).

117. *See* Keller v. Phillips, 39 N.Y. 351 (1868). A husband was liable for his wife's purchases even if some impediment to the marriage rendered it void. *See* Frank v. Carter, 219 N.Y. 35 (1916). But the wife's agency was a question of fact implied from the marriage relationship, *see* Wanamaker v. Weaver, 176 N.Y. 75 (1903), and could be rebutted by a showing that the husband had not authorized his wife to serve as his agent. *See* Kowing v. Manly, 49 N.Y. 192 (1872).

118. *See* Jones v. Walker, 63 N.Y. 612 (1875).

Conclusion: The Emergence of Policy-Oriented Judging

1. 1 Cranch (5 U.S.) 137 (1803).

2. *See generally* William E. Nelson, *E Pluribus Unum: How the Common Law Helped Unify and Liberate Colonial America, 1607–1776* (New York: Oxford University Press, 2018).

3. *See* William E. Nelson, *Marbury v. Madison: The Origins and Legacy of Judicial Review Second Edition, Revised and Expanded* (Lawrence: University Press of Kansas, 2018), 56–67.

4. 6 Mass. 401 (1810).

5. 14 Mass. 340 (1817).

6. *See* William E. Nelson, *Americanization of the Common Law: The Impact of Legal Change on Massachusetts Society, 1780–1830* (Cambridge, MA: Harvard University Press, 1975), 108–109.

7. *See* Wynehamer v. People, 13 N.Y. 378 (1856).

8. *See* Lemmon v. People, 20 N.Y. 562 (1860).

9. Oliver Wendell Holmes, "The Path of the Law," *Harvard Law Review* 10 (1897): 457.

10. Holmes, "The Path of the Law," 465–466.

11. Holmes, "The Path of the Law," 469.

12. Holmes, "The Path of the Law," 466.

13. Holmes, "The Path of the Law," 469.

14. Holmes, "The Path of the Law," 474.

15. Benjamin N. Cardozo, *The Nature of the Judicial Process* (New Haven, CT: Yale University Press, 1921).

16. Cardozo, *Nature of the Judicial Process*, 23.

17. Cardozo, *Nature of the Judicial Process*, 102.

18. Cardozo, *Nature of the Judicial Process*, 98.

19. Cardozo, *Nature of the Judicial Process*, 112–113.

20. Cardozo, *Nature of the Judicial Process*, 115.

21. 198 U.S. 45 (1905).

22. 217 N.Y. 382 (1916).

23. *Cf.* Citizens United v. Federal Election Comm'n, 558 U.S. 310 (2010).

24. 201 N.Y. 271 (1911).

25. 201 N.Y. at 292.

26. 201 N.Y. at 294.

27. *See* Jensen v. Southern Pacific Co., 215 N.Y. 514 (1915), *rev'd on other grounds*, Southern Pacific Co. v. Jensen, 244 U.S. 205 (1917).

28. 201 N.Y. 271, 285 (1911).

Index

www.ingramcontent.com/pod-product-compliance
Lightning Source LLC
Chambersburg PA
CBHW030943150426
42812CB00065B/3106/J